AMSTERDAM

the gloobles guide

AMSTERDAM

the gloobles guide

fourth edition

the idea behind it all

We have travelled to cities around the world, seeking out the most interesting, unique & delicious places wherever we go. And why, you ask? All in hopes of creating fun & functional guides for gloobles readers & passionate travellers. These guides are meticulously curated yet totally practical, with each & every tip being one of our very favourite spots. Our perfect trip is all about balance—we love cosy family-run shops & pocket-sized food stalls as much as grand, sweeping Michelin-starred restaurants & opulent hotels. We want places peddling quality wares that still have an eye toward the aesthetic.

Though we could have chosen a number of wonderful cities, we thought it was only right to start with our hometown, Amsterdam. AMSTERDAM *the gloobles guide* is not your everyday guidebook. It captures the energy & dynamism of one of the most fantastic cities we know, dishing on the best of the best of what to see & do for discerning flâneurs & locals alike. The ideal way to see a city is with a local. Travelling with AMSTERDAM *the gloobles guide* in your pocket is the next best thing.

Whether you are staying for just 24 hours or here for a week, getting down to business on a work trip or simply looking for a fresh perspective on your own city, this book is just what the doctor ordered. From intimate brown cafés to impressive museums, there is something for everyone, something that captures the *gezelligheid* of the city. Thoughtfully researched by the gloobles team & friends and illustrated by Sophia van den Hoek's original photography, AMSTERDAM *the gloobles guide* is everything you want a guidebook to be: useful, engaging & beautiful.

Amsterdam's charming canal houses seem to be leaning, but that's no accident! The tilt protects their facades during a move.

what's inside...

Amsterdam is divided into neighbourhoods that are simultaneously distinct and fluid. Check out our map to get a better feel for the city.

Amsterdam: the lowdown

Amsterdam is a city like no other. Canals weave in & out as seamlessly as the balletic bicyclists, and there is truly never a dull moment here. No matter the time of day, no matter the time of year, the city is cloaked in a particular, painterly light that has both travellers & locals scrambling for their phones to capture that perfect shot. *Echte Amsterdammers* are stylish yet approachable, serious yet quick to chuckle or wave you over to join them for a sip of jenever.

And that's before we even think about the vibrant expat community.

Whatever the reason is you're here—to sniff out the most incredible antiques, to lose yourself like Camus's Jean-Baptiste Clamence, to soak up the splendour of a lost age or simply to indulge in some good, old-fashioned hedonism—you are sure to find what you're looking for in droves. Amsterdam, 'Venice of the North', is a city that welcomes and captivates in equal measure. So even if you're here for only a little while, we are certain we will see you again very soon.

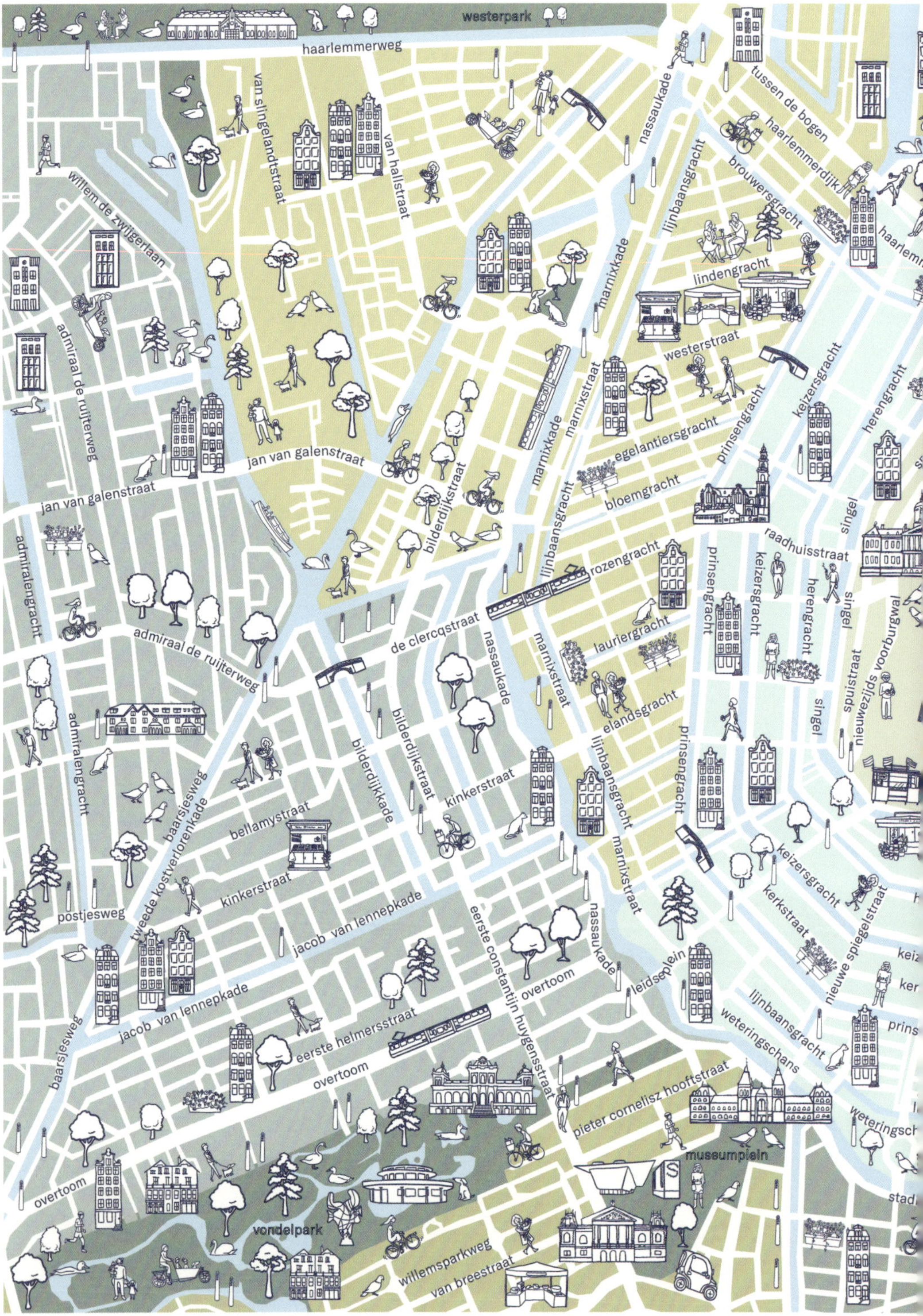
westerpark
haarlemmerweg
van slingelandtstraat
van hallstraat
nassaukade
tussen de bogen
haarlemmerdijk
brouwersgracht
lijnbaansgracht
willem de zwijgerlaan
marnixkade
lindengracht
westerstraat
admiraal de ruijterweg
marnixstraat
marnixkade
prinsengracht
keizersgracht
herengracht
egelantiersgracht
jan van galenstraat
jan van galenstraat
bilderdijkstraat
bloemgracht
raadhuisstraat
singel
admiralengracht
rozengracht
lijnbaansgracht
prinsengracht
keizersgracht
herengracht
singel
nieuwezijds voorburgwal
de clercqstraat
nassaukade
marnixstraat
lauriergracht
spuistraat
admiraal de ruijterweg
elandsgracht
singel
bilderdijkstraat
bilderdijkkade
kinkerstraat
lijnbaansgracht
prinsengracht
admiralengracht
baarsjesweg
tweede kostverlorenkade
bellamystraat
marnixstraat
kinkerstraat
keizersgracht
kerkstraat
nieuwe spiegelstraat
postjesweg
jacob van lennepkade
eerste constantijn huygensstraat
nassaukade
leidseplein
overtoom
jacob van lennepkade
lijnbaansgracht
weteringschans
eerste helmersstraat
overtoom
baarsjesweg
pieter cornelisz hooftstraat
museumplein
overtoom
vondelpark
willemsparkweg
van breestraat

ceramiquelaan
IJ-tunnel
meeuwenlaan
noordwal
sumatrakade
javakade
weemkade
piet heinkade
prins hendrikkade
stationplein
oosterdokskade
dijksgracht
zeedijk
prins hendrikkade
damrak
piet heinkade
kattenburgerstraat
oudezijds voorburgwal
oudezijds achterburgwal
sint antoniesbreestr.
oudeschans
grote wittenburgerstraat
nieuwe uilenburgerstraat
valkenburgerstraat
kloveniersburgwal
wittenburgergracht
conradstraat
entrepotdok
hoogte kadijk
mr. visserpl.
cruquiuskade
waterlooplein
hortus botanicus
rembrandtplein
artis
plantage middenlaan
zeeburgerdijk
herengracht
amstel
nieuwe keizersgracht
plantage muidergracht
sarphatistraat
mauritskade
reguliersgracht
weesperstraat
nieuwe prinsengracht
dapperstraat
linnaeusstraat
prinsengracht
sarphatistraat
amstel
oosterpark
frederikspl.
mauritskade
oosterpark
sarphatistraat
ruyschstraat
linnaeusstraat
weesperzijde
eerste oosterparkstraat
beukenweg
amsteldijk
populierenweg

going Dutch

"Discover
Amsterdam
by foot.
Strolling is
the best way
to find those
hidden spots
where only
locals go."

— Stephanie

how to get into town

by train
Taking the train is the cheapest way (€5) to get to & from Schiphol Airport—in just 15 minutes, you arrive at Amsterdam Centraal Station. If you're taking the Eurostar or another international train, this is also the station where you arrive.

by taxi
If you are looking for a more luxurious & relaxed way to get to your temporary home in Amsterdam, use the Uber app (€35) or the official taxi stand (€55) directly outside the arrivals hall. Ignore the opportunistic 'chauffeurs' lurking inside the arrivals hall at Schiphol Airport.

how to get around

by foot
The central city is relatively small, so it's easy to explore by foot. *Let op!* (that means be careful). Don't walk in the bike lane, and be sure to check both ways before you cross the street.

by bike
Amsterdam is remarkably flat, so bikes are our first choice for transport. In fact, there are actually more bikes than people here. If you can't beat 'em, join 'em! Don't forget to indicate where you're headed by sticking your hand out. Think of it as a Dutch turn signal. Be cautious of the tram rails, as it's easy for your wheel to get caught. There are plenty of rental shops around town, but Het Zwarte Fietsenplan will rent you a cool local bike so you don't stick out like a sore thumb. Be sure to lock your bike; thieves are everywhere!

by car
Driving in the centre is not advisable, but if you need to get somewhere quickly (or without getting soaked), use the Uber app for hassle-free hauling.

by public transport
Trams are easy and cover most of the city. Take the metro if you need to get from North to South or the other way around. Travelling by train is great when you're ready to venture out of the city. Buy a 1-4-day pass for unlimited tram, bus & metro rides if it's going to be rainy during your stay. Don't forget to check in & check out on the tram.

by boat
There is no more magical way to see the city than by boat. Rent your own from Sloepdelen or Mokumboat and pack a bottle or two & some Dutch delicacies. If the weather is awful—or you're a nervous captain—you can still catch the sights from the water by hopping on one of the many canal boat tours.

Learn how to blend in with the *Amsterdammers* →

how to blend in

meet & greet
When you meet somebody for the first time, shake their hand and introduce yourself by saying your first name. If you are meeting a friend, three kisses on the cheek is the way to go.

Dutch lessons

Dutch people are among the best non-native English speakers in the world, so you're unlikely to struggle here if you have a decent command of the language. That being said, Dutchies love when you make a bit of an effort with their language, so it never hurts to know a few key phrases.

gezellig /ɣəˈzɛ.ləx/
While there is no English equivalent, it roughly means cosy/warm/fun/sweet. Sheltering from the rain with a *biertje* in a brown bar is *gezellig*. When someone invites you for a cup of coffee, respond: *gezellig*. It's how locals convey a sense of happiness.

biertje /bɪɹtd͡ʒ/
This one is pretty self-explanatory, but it's also essential in this beer-drinking capital. Want just one? That's *een biertje*. Ordering for a friend? Ask the bartender for *twee biertjes alstublieft*.

dankjewel /ˌdɑŋk.jəˈʋɛl/
To thank someone in a casual way, you can say *dankjewel* or *dank je*. For a more formal expression of thanks, go with *dankuwel* or *bedankt*.

hoi /ɦɔi̯/
We bet you can guess what this one means. That's right! It's the way to say hi!

doei /dui̯/
There are many ways to say goodbye in Dutch, but *doei* is probably our favourite.

packing tips

This is a walking city with bridges & old streets, so comfortable sneakers are essential. Since it rains a lot, we also recommend packing an umbrella or a raincoat.

Dutch delicacies

avg'tje
The term for a classic Dutch dinner of potatoes, meat & veggies.

bitterballen
Delicious, deep-fried crispy ragout-balls traditionally served with mustard for dipping. They're the ultimate snack, and you can get them in every Dutch pub. Or head to the iconic FEBO for a croquette (the long version of a *bitterbal*).

drop
Dutch love their liquorice. It is not liquorice as you know it, so don't be shocked when you get hit by its intense salinity.

Dutch cheese
Holland is known for its cheese. Don't go home without visiting our favourite cheese shop Fromagerie Abraham Kef.

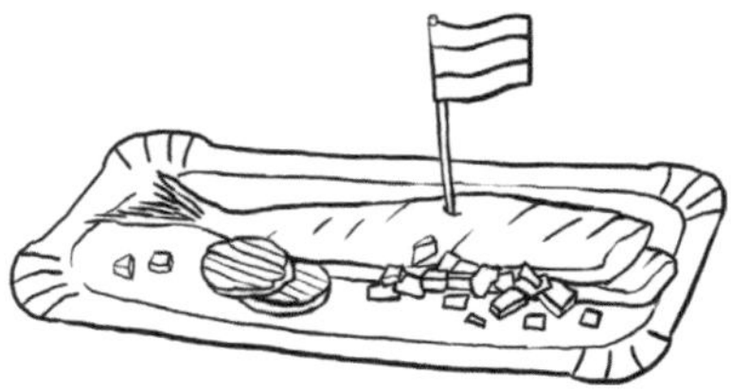

herring
You'll spot carts serving up this Dutch specialty all over the city, but Frens Haringhandel is our favourite of all. The best time to try raw herring is between May & July when the herring is the freshest & sweetest.

stroopwafel
Our favourite Dutch sweet treat. Two thin waffles stuck together with a layer of sugary syrup. You can buy them at any bakery or supermarket.

When should you visit Amsterdam? Continue reading →

what's on when

when to visit

Weather-wise, April through September is the best time to visit. The glorious outdoors are in full swing, which also means, the crowds are too. Winter can be chilly, grey & drizzly, but it's also cosy & often crowd-free.

Amsterdam events calendar

27 April
King's Day
This is probably the biggest holiday of the year in the Netherlands. King's Day (known as Queen's Day until recently) marks the birth of King Willem-Alexander and is celebrated on April 27th every year. Don't forget to wear orange!

4 & 5 May
Remembrance & Liberation Day
Remembrance Day & Liberation Day fall one day after the other in May. Remembrance Day commemorates those who have died in global conflicts, while Liberation Day celebrates the freedom from Nazi occupation after World War II. Everyone recognises a moment of silence at 8pm on the 4th.

June
Holland Festival
The Holland Festival is the oldest & largest performing arts festival in the Netherlands. You can expect music, theatre, opera, modern dance & more.

mid-June
Open Garden Days
For one weekend only, some of the most pristine gardens belonging to Amsterdam's finest canal houses swing open their doors for all to enjoy.

late July or early August
Pride Amsterdam
Sure, most cities have their own Pride celebrations, but nobody does it better than Amsterdam. The parade down the canals is joyful, inclusive and not to be missed.

Amsterdam events calendar continues on the next page →

mid-August
Grachtenfestival Amsterdam
This is truly one of the cultural highlights of the summer. The Grachtenfestival takes place on Amsterdam's most beautiful canals and focuses on the glories of classical music.

August
Vondelpark Open Air Theatre
Summer in Amsterdam is pretty unbeatable. Make the most of it by attending one of the seasonal concerts, comedy shows or dance performances at the Vondelpark Openluchttheater.

August
Lowlands
Held 68 kilometres east of Amsterdam, Lowlands is a cool music festival that's ideal for those who like to camp. It's won awards for the Best Overseas Festival, so you know it's worth it.

September
Dutch Grand Prix in Zandvoort
Forget France. The Netherlands is where it's at when it comes to Formula 1 racing if you ask us. With 32 races under its belt since the first race back in 1950, the Zandvoort circuit is known for legendary races and pulsating energy.

October
Amsterdam Dance Event (ADE)
Anyone who's into electronic music has probably already heard of ADE. But even if you're not a total fangirl (or boy), you are sure to enjoy the energy that courses through the city during this weekend in October.

November
Museum Night
As you might have noticed, Amsterdam is known for its museums, but there's something extra special about seeing those historic sites in a new light. After dark, that is! One wristband gets you access to over 50 museums – both special exhibitions & the permanent collections – until 2am.

late November
International Documentary Festival (IDFA)
When the rest of the world starts to quiet down, Amsterdam only amps things up. November shines bright in Amsterdam, thanks to the IDFA, the world's largest documentary film festival.

early December
Amsterdam Light Festival
See the city sparkle & come alive as everything from buildings to bridges glitters with spectacular light installations.

CENTRUM

Centrum is one of Amsterdam's busiest neighbourhoods, so we like to explore on foot, leaving our bikes at home.

GET TO KNOW CENTRUM

Tucked away in the arms of the world-famous Canal Ring, Centrum is Amsterdam's historical city centre. This innermost borough might be the first bit of Amsterdam you see if you arrive by train, as Centraal Station is at the very tippy top of the neighbourhood, overlooking the IJ.

The city unfolds organically, with charming, typically Dutch buildings at every turn. They teeter precariously over a maze of canals, playing host to fantastic museums like Ons' Lieve Heer op Solder, glittering shops like Lyppens and restaurants you will go back to time and time again. Oh, we could not possibly forget about the Red Light District. It may not be your daily haunt, but it is something everyone must see at least once (or twice!) in their lives.

Athena de Belder

gloobles curator Centrum

This Belgian beauty is already a travel guru in her own right, cataloguing her stunning, adventurous travels on her carefully curated Instagram. Though she now works in Amsterdam, she's lived all over, from London to New York & many, many places in between. When we're looking for the best workout in town or the most beautiful spot for coffee & cake, we know we can always ask Athena!

"When I tell people I live in Centrum, they immediately say: but is it not too busy?"

That's also the first thing I asked myself when I moved from Oud-West to Centrum in 2021. Funnily enough, it's turned out to be more peaceful than I could have imagined. Life in Centrum feels a little more relaxed since you tend to walk everywhere rather than cycle. If you wake up early enough (any time before 8:00 on weekdays and 10:00 on weekends), you have Grachtengordel and *De Negen Straatjes* pretty much to yourself. And, aside from visiting tourists, it's pretty much all locals who've been around for decades living in the centre.

I love having a little chat with them as they go about their days. There are four women I see every morning, bundled up in robes with goggles on their heads, who meet up for a dip in the canal; I greet them as I take off for my morning workout. It's these small interactions that make me love the city more every day.

There's no better way to start the day than with a workout (at least in my book!). Some favourites include the high intensity cycling workouts at Rocycle, Hot Pilates at Movements and hot yoga at Equal. For a workout with the best view, I'll go to the Soho House gym or go for a swim on the rooftop.

On the weekends, I like to get myself a little post-workout treat, and I often opt for a croissant. One of my favourite bakeries in Centrum is Gebroeders Niemeijer. They have all the French classics like sourdough baguettes, cannelés, tarte tatin and small but mighty croissants. After grabbing a few treasures from Niemeijer, I'll head toward the edge of Centrum to stop by my favourite independent book and magazine shop, Athenaeum. After a long day of work, I love to unwind with a glass of chilled wine in one hand and a snack in the other.

To me, living in buzzing Centrum is all about finding little pockets of peace, whether that's a quiet stroll in the morning past the historical canal houses or sitting down at one of the many cafés with a book, watching the world pass by.

Julia Khan Anselmo

gloobles curator Centrum

It's rare that someone integrates so fully into a city that you'd have a hard time imagining it without them. Julia has proved that, sometimes, an outsider is really the most insider of all. Building community is at the core of what Julia does. She hosts supper clubs, curates events, teaches workshops and creates beautiful things—online and in person—for her brand Feisty Feast. When we're with Julia, life just feels more enchanting.

"I love wandering through the neighbourhood and discovering all these charming nooks and crannies I didn't know existed."

My fiancée and I bought our house back in 2021. It's this beautiful old spice merchant's home at the crossing of the Prins Hendrikkade and the Peperstraat. After two years of renovations, we finally finished; while it was a lot of hard work, we are thrilled with how things have turned out.

Our neighbourhood is in one of the older, more established parts of the city. A lot of our neighbours have been living here for years and years, and they're all really lovely. This part of Centrum has that true neighbourhood feel, where people are living together in a sort of community. Our neighbours Rudolph and Hylkia often have us over for dinner, and we are so grateful to have been welcomed the way we have.

When you slow down and hop off your bike–which most of us rarely do here in Amsterdam–there's so much to see, especially in Centrum. I love wandering through the neighbourhood and discovering all these charming nooks and crannies I didn't know existed. It's nice because the area still isn't saturated, so there's so much room for new things to pop up and things to grow and evolve.

Our house is really close to Hiding in Plain Sight, an exceptional hidden cocktail bar, and Gebroeders Hartering. Sometimes, we'll go for dinner there, and sometimes a friend will simply pass by and grab a bottle of their beautiful old-world wine or two on the way to our place for dinner. The Waterlooplein, with plenty of stalls of vintage clothing and antiques, is also just around the corner.

Recently, I discovered Café Schiller in the Rembrandtplein. Right in the middle of this touristy square, you suddenly have this beautiful gem of an art deco restaurant. You feel as if you're stepping back in time into a classic French bistro. It's refreshingly different from this whole natural-wine-small-plates trend.

One of the best things about Centrum is how close you are to the Amstel. I love going for a long walk or hopping on my bike and heading out into Oude Kerk. It really feels like you're in the countryside.

Living in Centrum definitely isn't something we planned to do–we really chose it because of the house–but we are so happy it's where we've ended up. It's a bit residential, it's close to everything you want to do in the city and, best of all, there's always something new to discover.

de ruijterkade
haarlemmerstraat
prins hendrikkade
keizersgracht
herengracht
singel
spuistraat
damrak
oudezijds voorburgwal
zeedijk
prins hendrikkade
oosterdokskade
kloveniersburgwal
sint antoniesbreestr.
oudeschans
nieuwe uilenburgerstr.
valkenburgerstraat
hoogte kadijk
entrepotdok
mr. visserpl.
waterlooplein
hortus botanicus
herengracht
singel
singel
herengracht
muntpl.
amstel
rembrandtplein
plantage middenlaan
plantage muidergracht
nieuwe spiegelstraat
keizersgracht
kerkstraat
prinsengracht
reguliersgracht
prinsengracht
weesperstraat
nieuwe prinsengracht
amstel
sarphatistraat
frederikspl.
lijnbaansgracht
weteringschans
mauritskade
1&2
3
4
5
6
7
8
9
10
11
12
13
14
15
16
17
18
19
20

CENTRUM

get sleepy

sleep. coffee. lunch. drinks. dinner.

De L'Europe

Perched on a prominent corner of the Amstel, De L'Europe is an easy walk from both the museums & *De Negen Straatjes*. Recently renovated, the interior is just as awe-inspiring as the exterior, so you may be tempted to ditch cultural plans in favour of a day cosied up in your luxurious room. Our favourite part? Brasserie Marie. Great views. Great food. Great!

Nieuwe Doelenstraat 2-14
+31 20 531 1777

sleep.

gloobles suite at De L'Europe

Are we ok with a little self-promotion? Yeahhhhh, we think so. Especially since we're convinced our suite at Hotel de L'Europe is probably the coolest place to kip in all of Amsterdam. Explore everything the city has to offer with both our out-of-suite experiences (think: a tip treasure hunt around town) and in-room amenities in stunning Suite 152.

Nieuwe Doelenstraat 2-14
+31 20 531 1777

sleep. drinks. beauty. work.

Soho House

If you've been in any major city in the past five or ten years, then you have certainly heard of Soho House. The Amsterdam outpost of this hip, international chain is just as cool and thoughtfully decorated as the rest. The rooms are relatively reasonably priced, and there's a gym, movie theatre & rooftop pool to make your stay all that much more exciting.

Spuistraat 210
+31 20 888 0300

get lunch

“If you’re looking for a proper brunch that’s still a bit peaceful, head to @droog Amsterdam.”

— Athena

coffee. lunch. culture.

@droog Amsterdam

Functioning as a café, library and art space, @droog has a little something for everyone–particularly the creatively inclined. Keep an eye on their website for upcoming events and collaborations!

Staalstraat 7b
Monday-Sunday 11am-5pm
+31 20 217 0100

coffee. lunch.

Gartine

Though the Brits have definitely laid claim to high tea, it turns out the Dutch can do it just as well…if not a little bit better. If we're winding our way through the narrow streets in Centrum, we always make a point to stop in at Gartine for a light breakfast or their afternoon tea with a Dutch twist. It doesn't hurt that everything on the menu is homemade & organic.

Taksteeg 7
Wednesday-Friday 9.30am-5pm
& Saturday-Sunday 9am-4pm
+31 20 320 4132

Les vins de Champagne
BOLLINGER
KRUG
ICE BOX
ICE BOX
ICE BOX
BOLLINGER

get drinks

drinks. dinner.

Bar du Champagne

The busiest (and often most touristy) parts of Amsterdam tend to be places we avoid at all costs. And while you'll never find us barrelling through the flower market or queueing at Madame Tussaud's, you almost certainly will spot us heading down the Rokin on our way to the charming Bar du Champagne. This small cellar bar serves excellent Champagnes and churns out masterful small bites—just what we've been missing.

Rokin 91a
Monday 4-11pm & Wednesday-Friday 4-11pm
& Saturday 12-11pm
+31 20 737 3194

get dinner

dinner.

Choux

For years, people have slighted vegetables. Thankfully, that's no longer the case, particularly at Choux. This trendy restaurant near Centraal Station gives prominence to the humble vegetable. The menu is ever-changing, and the kitchen prides itself on employing as many local, seasonal products as possible. Come to Choux to be delighted by the wonders of the earth.

De Ruijterkade 128
Tuesday-Saturday 6pm-12am
+31 20 210 3090

dinner.

Gebroeders Hartering

This cosy, intimate restaurant in Amsterdam's Rapenburg is all about using seasonal products from local craft suppliers—plus, they offer prime seating on their boat just outside the restaurant. If that isn't tempting enough, their focus on top-notch wine pairings should be sufficient to lure you inside. Though they're not open for lunch, the kitchen is still churning out delicious food until quite late, so it's a great spot to pop into after the ballet or opera.

Peperstraat 10
Monday-Sunday 6-10pm
+31 20 421 0699

drinks. dinner.

Trees

Named after a fabulous femme who used to pound the streets of Centrum for decades, enchanting everyone she passed, Trees is set to become the same kind of household name quite quickly. And not just in the neighbourhood. Flattering lighting, warm wood pannelling and a menu that feels simultaneously accessible and special, Geza Weisz's latest outpost is just wonderful.

Zeedijk 14a
Tuesday-Thursday 5.30pm-12am
& Friday-Saturday 5.30pm-1am
+31 20 280 1334

get shopping

shop.

Athenaeum Boekhandel & Nieuwscentrum

Although we are always on the go, we are never without a book, stashed away in our bags or tucked into a (roomy) pocket. When we want a little guidance for finding inspiring books or want the best magazines, there's only one place we ever go: Athenaeum Boekhandel & Nieuwscentrum. Looking for a paper to enjoy while you luxuriate over a coffee at Café de Pels or Screaming Beans? There's a great selection here.

Spui 14-16
Monday-Saturday 10am-7pm & Sunday 11am-7pm
+31 20 514 1460

shop.

De Bijenkorf

Despite its diminutive size, Amsterdam has everything to offer that a bigger capital would: great nightlife, fantastic restaurants and, of course, a glittering, impressive department store. London can keep Harrods; let Paris have Le Bon Marché. Because we have De Bijenkorf. Carve out a few hours to wind your way through the cavernous space and find something that really speaks to you.

Dam 1
Monday-Saturday 10am-9pm & Sunday 10am-8pm
+31 20 808 9333

shop. lunch.

Dun Yong Kitchen & Shop

For years, Dun Yong has been on our bi-weekly grocery route thanks to their incredible selection of goodies from China, Japan, Vietnam, India and beyond. After we've finished our haul, we like to climb the stairs up to the restaurant to indulge in some umami-packed yakisoba and okonomiyaki. Oh! And Chef Taka's ramen, of course.

Stormsteeg 9
Monday-Friday 9am-7pm & Saturday 9am-6pm
& Sunday 11am-6pm
+31 20 261 7689

shop.

Filling Pieces

Though we're obviously pretty global here at gloobles, we've got to admit that we really love when we see our beloved Dutch brands shining on the international stage. One very cool brand doing just that is Filling Pieces. Bridging cultural gaps, Filling Pieces is a brand that speaks to just about everyone—hypebeasts, the streetwear savvy, classic cool kids & traditionalists alike.

Spuistraat 168a
Monday 12-7pm & Tuesday-Saturday 11am-7pm
& Sunday 12-6pm
+31 20 280 1866

> "This hidden gem is just wonderful – even if you're only looking."
>
> — Julia

shop.

Lyppens

You know what they say. Diamonds are a girl's best friend. We like to think they're everyone's best friend. Well, sapphires as well. Wait, we can't forget about emeralds. Basically, we love everything at this famous Dutch jeweller. Not in the market for new or vintage jewels? You can also sell your old pieces here and put the money toward whatever tickles your fancy.

Langebrugsteeg 8
Tuesday-Saturday 10am-6pm by appointment
+31 20 627 0901

get beautiful

beauty.

Cowshed Spa

Massages. Pedicures. Full beard shapes. Name a treatment, and you can likely find it at this gorgeous, relaxing spa tucked away inside Soho House. This lovely spa is small, with only six treatment rooms, so be sure to book ahead if you want to get a spot. If you're feeling extra indulgent, you can book the Relax & Refuel, which includes a massage & a two-course lunch at Cecconi's every Tuesday to Thursday.

Soho House, Spuistraat 210
Monday-Sunday 9am-8pm
+31 20 888 0300

get cultured

culture.

Dutch National Opera & Ballet

This stunning building, gracefully situated on the Amstel, is home to the world-renowned Dutch National Opera & Dutch National Ballet. You can, of course, find age-old classics performed here, but we're particularly enchanted by their unique, progressive productions. They have an ever-changing roster of performances, so it's wise to check their website for their current programme.

Amstel 3
doors open an hour before the performance
+31 20 625 5455

IHS

culture.

Ons' Lieve Heer op Solder

It might sound a bit hyperbolic, particularly when you see all the other incredible buildings in Amsterdam, but this is probably one of the most beautiful & Instagrammable places in the whole city. This 17th-century canal house has its very own chapel that just so happens to be bright pink. This is a photo opportunity that can't be missed.

Oudezijds Voorburgwal 38-40
Monday-Sunday 10am-6pm
+31 20 624 6604

culture.

Secret Garden at Nicolas Groente & Fruit

From the outside, Nicholas Groente & Fruit seems like nothing more than a simple, albeit charming, neighbourhood grocer on a little street in Centrum. Head inside, through the shop and then outside once again, and you'll realise it's much, much more. Nicholas Groente & Fruit's secret garden is home to works by some of the best street artists in the Netherlands. Grab your weekly groceries and see striking street art 'in the wild'.

Nicholas Groente & Fruit, Sint Nicolaasstraat 19
Tuesday 1-8pm & Wednesday-Sunday 12-8pm
+31 62 715 6164

DON'T LET
FUTURE
HOLD
BACK
MATH!

DE JORDAAN & WESTERPARK

On sunny Saturdays, you can find us zipping through De Jordaan,
picking up provisions for a picnic in the Westerpark.

GET TO KNOW DE JORDAAN & WESTERPARK

Built in the early 17th century, De Jordaan is one of the most beautiful corners of the city. Though it was originally a working class *buurt* that played host to a wildly diverse population of immigrants, the area is now one of the most 'Amsterdam' neighbourhoods there is. As you trot across the charming *grachten* that zigzag through De Jordaan, you'll notice many of the streets bearing the names of beautiful fauna. Some say that's why it's called De Jordaan, claiming it comes from the French word for garden, *jardin*. Even further afield is Westerpark, but it is no less charming. In fact, some of our very favourite spots happen to be there!

Whenever we're in Westerpark or De Jordaan, we love diving deep into the incredible markets, always coming out with a treasure or two. We never miss a chance to grab an espresso at T O K I (and a piece of Dutch apple pie at Winkel 43) before hunting for the best cotton cashmere at Khasto. Still around when the sun is setting? Pop into Bar Parry for unusual wines & creative small bites.

Lukas Lewandowski

gloobles curator De Jordaan & Westerpark

A true multi-hyphenate, Lukas has lived many lives. Stylist. Chef. Creative. Psychologist. He's done it all. Lukas ping-pongs between his apartment in Amsterdam, his guesthouse and creative residency in Sicily (Casa Lawa, here we come!) and the home where he grew up in Poland. But if you can't find him in any of those spots, you can bet he's on the road, capturing his travels with his Olympus Mju and in his memory-delicious bites, beaches and all.

"I have grown to be a little sentimental about this place."

On my perfect Saturday morning, I wake up, make a huge coffee and have my sweet-savoury granola with tons of nuts, nice Greek yoghurt & fresh fruit. I'll sit down and make a little grocery list for that evening's supper. Sweet. Then, I'll head to De Noordermarkt to score some goodies. My first stop, a cheese stall with all kinds of cheese. Danish, Swiss, Dutch, French, Spanish, Portuguese, British. Even this amazing cheddar with truffle - my secret for the best omelette ever. My favourite vegetable stands are there, as well as van Menno. I adore their baguette with black olives; it's perfect for sandwiches. Oh! And there's also this great stall, Bellemarie, that sells herbs, edible flowers & homemade pestos. They have rare ingredients that are tough to find anywhere else in the city.

There is a beautiful shop on the corner called De Oliewinkel that sells olive oil, vinegars, olives & all these nice little delicacies. My absolute fave is this green earthy olive oil from Tuscany. They always let you taste whatever you want.

Sometimes, instead of going to De Noordermarkt, I'll join a vinyasa class at the yoga studio I've been going to for years, Svaha. It's been open for decades and is run by a couple, Patrick and Gosta. They met in New York in the nineties, returned to Amsterdam and opened this wonderful studio.

Around the corner, there's my favourite dry cleaner, Rio. They've saved me from a lot of red wine stains over the years. They fix everything - even the unfixable. It feels like a very adult thing to mention, but they've been my saviours.

If I don't have breakfast at home, I love going to d&a hummus bistro. It's easygoing, honest food. Everyone who works there is so lovely.

After lunch, I'll probably grab a coffee at TOKI. I have grown to be a little sentimental about this place. They stole my heart when I found out they have the Heim Söhne spoons I collect. There is a very cute shop called DEKSELS! on the Haarlemmerdijk; they have great non-stick pans, spatulas & literally everything my cooking soul desires. Next door is a shop packed with cookbooks. I bought all of mine there, and some of them have even come to Casa Lawa with me. Usually, I like to develop my rolls of film on Saturdays, so I'll head to Foto Den Boer. Then I'll probably go home to start to work on dinner for family & friends, who usually come early with a good bottle of wine. We'll snack on the bread from De Noordermarkt and some olives, dipping the bread in olive oil, nibbling on Comté and spreading some tapenades while I cook.

nova zemblastraat
van diemenstraat
spaarndammerstraat
zaanstraat
planciusstraat
prinseneiland
grote bickersstraat
westerdoksdijk
haarlemmerweg
de wittenkade
nassaukade
lijnbaansgracht
brouwersgracht
haarlemmerdijk
marnixkade
lindengracht
westerstraat
marnixstraat
bilderdijkstraat
prinsengracht
keizersgracht
herengracht
singel
spuistraat
egelantiersgracht
bloemgracht
raadhuisstraat
rozengracht
lauriergracht
nieuwezijds voorburgwal
kinkerstraat
1
2
3
4
5
6
7
8
9
10
11
12
13
14
15
16
17
18
19
20
21
22
23
24
25
26
27
28
29
30
31
32

DE JORDAAN & WESTERPARK

get breakfast

breakfast. coffee. lunch. takeout. shop.

Breadwinner

Breadwinner is, dare we say, a real winner when it comes to breakfast in the 'dam. Opened by expats (so, you know they know a good schmear), this tiny sourdough microbakery churns out THE best bagels in the city. Bite into an everything bagel with cream cheese while you're there, then order one of their bagel BLTs to-go. Lunch sorted.

Tweede Laurierdwarsstraat 50hs
Wednesday 11am-3pm & Thursday-Sunday 9.30am-3pm

BREAD WINNER
This week's menu:
- BLT
- ALT
- Choc chip, nutella

get coffee

coffee. takeout.

TOKI

These days, most coffee spots start to feel the same, but thankfully not T O K I. With terrazzo everything & perfectly foamed lattes, this place is totally Instagrammable. But luckily style & substance go hand-in-hand at T O K I. The coffee & pastries are excellent, and the vibe is great. Bring your laptop or a book and settle in for the day.

Binnen Dommersstraat 15
Monday-Friday 8am-5pm
& Saturday-Sunday 9am-5pm

coffee.

Winkel 43

You may think it's American, but apple pie is about as Dutch as you can get. It may take a few extra minutes waiting in line at Winkel 43, but we promise it is totally worth the wait. It tends to be extra busy on Saturdays when De Noordermarkt is heaving with visitors, so sneak by for a slice of the best apple pie in the city on a quiet weekday afternoon.

Noordermarkt 43
Monday 7-1am & Tuesday-Thursday 8-1am & Friday 8-3am & Saturday 7-3am & Sunday 9-1am
+31 20 623 0223

get lunch

lunch. drinks. dinner.

Chez Nina

When we first heard that Chez Nina was a self-dubbed 'green brasserie', we must admit we were a little dubious. But boy, were we wrong! The dishes here are as inventive as they are delicious. Though everything is veg-focused, nothing is precious, and you most definitely won't finish your meal and find yourself hungry 45 minutes later. Chez Nina, we love you.

Van Limburg Stirumplein 10a
Monday-Friday 5.30pm-12am & Saturday-Sunday 12pm-12am
+31 62 883 6136

lunch. dinner. takeout.

Foodware

It can be tough to find a place for takeaway that isn't disgusting, disgustingly unhealthy or, worse, both. Foodware to the rescue! We love popping into this cute spot on the Looiersgracht to grab wholesome yet delicious food that's prepared fresh each day. Pick out your ideal meal and seek out a nearby bench in the sun for an impromptu picnic.

Looiersgracht 12
Monday-Saturday 12-9pm
+31 20 620 8898

get drinks

drinks.

Bar Parry

Tucked away on an intimate little side street in De Jordaan is this lovely, intimate wine bar—the little sister of Balthazar's Keuken. The incredibly friendly staff will gently guide you through the spectacular wine list and suggest the best of their delicious small plates to go along with whatever you decide to sip. No matter your choice, you are sure to be pleasantly surprised. We particularly love the sardines & the roasted leeks.

Eerste Looiersdwarsstraat 15
Wednesday 5-11pm & Thursday 5pm-12am
& Friday-Saturday 5pm-1am & Sunday 4-8pm
+31 20 334 8578

drinks. dinner.

R. de Rosa

When a neighbourhood bands together to create a community space, you can't always guarantee it's going to be good. R. de Rosa, however, is so good that it's not just a local beloved by residents of the Boomstraat. No! This charming corner café is always heaving with people from across the city. Grab a table outside and immediately understand why.

Boomstraat 41a
Wednesday-Thursday 3-11pm & Friday 3pm-12am
& Saturday 11am-12pm & Sunday 3-11pm

get dinner

dinner. takeout.

Akitsu

You'll forget all about bikes and *bitterballen* as soon as you cross the threshold at Akitsu, one of the best Japanese restaurants in town. They have a broad menu of yakitori, sushi, warm dishes and more, and they do just about everything very, very well (including takeaway!). Though it's not the most comfortable seat in the house, we love booking one of the traditional low tables. Shoes off, snacks on!

Rozengracht 228-230
Tuesday-Saturday 6-10pm
+31 20 625 3254

"The somewhat-hidden location adds a touch of adventure."

— Lukas

lunch. dinner.

BAK

From the outside, BAK doesn't look like much. But once you take the stairs up to the third floor of this stripped back, unassuming warehouse and step inside, you'll see what all the fuss is about. This industrial-style restaurant overlooking the former timber port of Amsterdam serves up a delicious vegetable-focused tasting menu. Ask for a table by the window to best enjoy the exceptional views & tasty bites.

Van Diemenstraat 408
Wednesday-Friday 6-10pm
& Saturday-Sunday 12.30-3pm, 6-10pm
+31 20 737 2553

dinner.

Balthazar's Keuken

People always say that good things come in small packages. Nowhere is that truer than at Balthazar's Keuken, a lovely, compact little restaurant on the Elandsgracht that we just can't help but frequent. The same certainly goes for sister spot Bar Parry. Ever since they opened back in 1995, Balthazar's Keuken has been serving a delicious & affordable tasting menu beloved by locals.

Elandsgracht 108
Wednesday-Sunday 6-11pm
+31 20 420 2114

lunch. drinks. dinner.

Café Parlotte

Parlotte is a supremely charming bistro & wine bar tucked away on Westerstraat. Why do we like Parlotte? It's a place where you can eat just as well as you drink (and trust us, that's very well – Margot, the sommelier, previously headed up wines at Café de Klepel). It's a spot that suits whatever you're in the market for.

Westerstraat 182
Monday 4pm-1am & Wednesday-Friday 4pm-1am
& Saturday 1pm-1am & Sunday 1-9pm
+31 62 530 5030

lunch. drinks. dinner.

calisto

With 10 simple but solid guest rooms and a menu made up of comforting but light Italian fare, calisto is sure to be soon cemented in the hearts of *Amsterdammers*. And visitors too, naturally. Housed in a monumental 17th-century building in the heart of De Jordaan, this guesthouse-cum-restaurant is another absolute smasher from Bob Nagel (of café binnenvisser & café twee prinsen) and his team.

Haarlemmerdijk 61
Monday-Friday 6pm-12am
& Saturday-Sunday 1-3:30pm, 6pm-12am

lunch. dinner.

Domenica

Though it's got seriously impressive credentials–both the chef & sommelier were at Toscanini for years–Domenica is totally down to earth. This homey, cosy spot is ideal for Sunday dinners (*domenica*, in Italian!) but is just as lovely any day of the week. With a little bit of Italian flair & a lot of warmth, Domenica is quickly becoming an old standby in our dining routine.

Noordermarkt 7
Tuesday-Saturday 12.30-2.30pm, 6-10pm
& Saturday 12-10pm & Sunday 12-4pm
+31 20 774 6720

lunch. dinner. takeout. shop.

Toscanini & Toscanini Deli

Toscanini is one of the true stalwarts of Amsterdam's fine dining scene, and it also happens to be our favourite Italian in town. It is the ideal place to celebrate a special occasion, though who's to say any old Tuesday night is not special enough? Take a peek into the open kitchen to watch the chefs work their magic. In the mood for something more casual? Grab a focaccia from their sister spot Toscanini Deli next door.

Lindengracht 75
Restaurant Toscanini: Monday-Thursday 6-11.30pm
& Friday-Saturday 12pm-1am
Toscanini Deli: Monday-Friday 11am-7pm
& Saturday 10am-6pm & Sunday 11am-6pm
+31 20 623 2813

get shopping

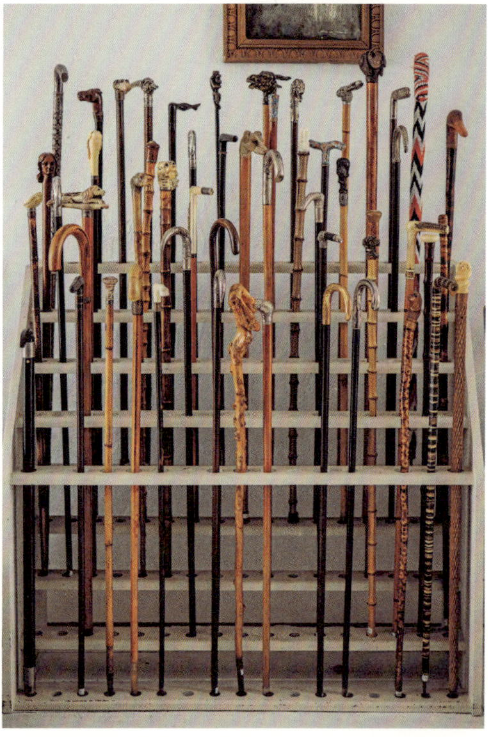

shop.

Antiek 58

Our only complaint about diminutive Antiek 58 is that it's only open once a week! But, man, are those Saturdays glorious! Cruising through De Jordaan on your bike, it'd be easy to miss this little shop, as it's almost hidden amidst the beautiful canal houses on either side. Johan, Antiek 58's proprietor, is incredibly knowledgeable about every piece and always open to a little bargaining.

Bloemgracht 58
Saturday 12-6pm
+31 68 134 9510

shop.

Au Paradis

Purity & originality are qualities that characterise each & every wine you find at Au Paradis. Like many blossoming wine shops these days, Au Paradis focuses on biodynamic wines. This is not any old natural wine store, however. Au Paradis serves up gorgeous bottles of only the most special French wines that all shout their terroir from the rooftops. *Très bien, non?*

Lindengracht 195
Tuesday-Friday 12-6.30pm & Saturday 12-6pm
+31 65 765 7227

Quinoa
Rood
500 gr. 4.40
Spelt
500 gr.
mung
bonen
500 gr.
310

takeout. shop.

De Noordermarkt

Every Saturday without fail, you will inevitably find us with a few canvas tote bags absolutely bursting with organic fresh produce & gourmet delicacies. Where have we been, you ask? Why, at De Noordermarkt, of course! Come early to ensure that you get the best pick of local breads, cheeses & vegetables. If you're not big on munchable delights, there are also many stalls peddling vintage furs & antique trinkets.

Noordermarkt
Saturday 9am-4pm

shop.

Khasto

When you're living in (or merely visiting) a city that's as chilly as Amsterdam for so much of the year, you've got to outfit your wardrobe with lots of beautiful, warm textiles. Khasto is a great shop that sells lovely handmade cotton-cashmere, from pyjamas to throw blankets to wraps. Pick up one of their adorable face masks for the flight home and thank us later.

Prinsengracht 272
Monday-Sunday 11am-6pm
+31 20 770 7340

shop.

Misc Store

Razor-sharp Japanese clippers! Milky cerulean pens! Patterned washi tape! Inspiring coffee table books! Cute crafty bits! Misc Store is the gift that keeps on giving and giving and giving. Though we're not always in NEED of anything they stock, we've never left without a little somethin' somethin'. Certainly one to add to your list.

Elandsgracht 59
Monday-Saturday 10:30am-6pm & Sunday 12-6pm
+31 20 700 9855

shop.

POMPON

On occasion, we definitely like to hit up De Noordermarkt or the Lindenmarkt for our flowers, but unfortunately, they're not available every day. When we just can't wait for a beautiful bouquet any longer, we make sure to head to POMPON, one of the loveliest flower shops in Amsterdam. It's particularly fantastic if you are feeling overwhelmed with options, as the friendly & knowledgeable staff will help you assemble the perfect bouquet. For something that lasts a little bit longer, check out their stunning shop next door for artfully crafted fake flowers.

Prinsengracht 8-12hs
(Fresh flowers) Tuesday-Saturday 10am-6pm
(Forever flowers) Wednesday-Friday 10am-6pm
& Saturday 10am-5pm
+31 20 622 5137

shop.

Tableware Amsterdam

Magpies, consummate hosts and antique aficionados will have a whale of a time at Tableware Amsterdam. Vintage glassware in dazzling colourways, antique silver napkin rings and kitsch crockery line the shelves (and the floors! and the tables!) at this chaotic but cute dreamland. Watch your step as you navigate the shop, as 'you break it, you buy it' is the motto here.

Eerste Tuindwarsstraat 1
Tuesday-Saturday 11am-5pm

shop.

Tenue de Nîmes

You are guaranteed to find something that tickles your fancy at Tenue de Nîmes. This gorgeous concept store stocks covetable clothes from labels like Acne Studios & Levi's and offers tailoring right on the spot. Though Amsterdam can be tricky for finding stylish clothing, you definitely won't leave Tenue de Nîmes empty-handed.

Elandsgracht 60
Monday 12-7pm & Tuesday-Friday 11-7pm
& Saturday 10am-6pm & Sunday 12-6pm
+31 20 320 4012

shop.

Time & Style

It's quite nice when things do exactly as they say on the label. Time & Style does just that. This beautiful boutique has a collection of stylish, timeless pieces for the home. Get ready to channel the supremely chic essence of Japan right here in Amsterdam.

Marnixstraat 148
Monday-Saturday 10am-6pm
+31 20 210 3176

shop.

Troppo Giovane

Too young. Too young! The owners of Troppo Giovane (which translates to "too young" in Italian) declared. The team at this super cool yet very friendly wine shop wants to encourage drinkers to move away from the newness that's popular in many wine stores and embrace true ageworthy bottles. Their selection focuses on Italian and French producers, but they've also got a nice, tight selection of orange wines, sake, mezcal and cider.

Binnen Dommersstraat 22-24
Tuesday-Friday 12-7.30pm & Saturday 10.30am-7.30pm
+31 64 991 9574

get creative

creativity.

Playhood

Grab the kiddos and scoot over to Houthavens. Playhood is calling! Every corner at this indoor play studio is adorable through and through. From Albert Klein to Dinky Kappers to Milky Bakery, it doesn't get any cuter than this. Sip a coffee with the other parents at the café whilst you let your kiddos' imaginations run wild.

Danzigerbocht 15
opening hours vary, so check the website for this week's schedule

get active

activity.

Rocycle – Centrum

Even if you already feel like you spend all your time glued to your bicycle seat here in Amsterdam, we strongly urge you to book a class at Rocycle. This boutique fitness studio brings you an energetic 45-minute full-body workout that is truly a party on a bike. Once you've sweated and cycled your heart out, you can grab a juice or a bracing ginger shot around the corner at Juice Brothers to bring you back to life.

Nieuwe Passeerdersstraat 12
For this week's schedule, check out their website
+31 20 369 7074

activity.

Westerpark

Sure, Amsterdam has no shortage of great parks that are perfect for whiling away an afternoon in the sun, but we couldn't possibly leave out the Westerpark. In addition to its expanses of leafy green space, the Westerpark also has a lively creative & nightlife scene. Pop into De Westergasfabriek to check out indie shops, a cinema & cool restaurants.

Westerpark
open all day, every day

get beautiful

beauty.

OJAI

More than "just a spa", OJAI is a place to rewind, recharge and, on a good day, come out feeling reborn. Alisa and her team perform what feels like miracle work with facial massage, highly refined facial treatments and wonderful alternative therapies like acupuncture and scalp treatments. If you want to look 10 years younger, splurge on a package of PRX facials.

Eerste Boomdwarsstraat 10h
Monday-Friday 9am-6pm & Saturday 10am-6pm
& Sunday 12-6pm
+31 61 546 2787

beauty.

Sun for Soul

It's relatively easy to feel relatively good in a city like Amsterdam. You're on your bike (active, check!). You've got access to a boon of produce (healthy eating, check!). But sometimes, you still feel a little out of whack. Jennifer Sun, the powerhouse behind Sun for Soul, is here to change that. She couples Traditional Chinese Medicine practices with acupuncture, cupping and a modern 'tude in order to help and heal Amsterdammers from tip to toe.

Willemsstraat 171
by appointment only
+31 62 138 8907

get cultured

culture.

The Movies

When you're going to the movies, now you can really go to *The Movies*. We adore this arthouse cinema, which just so happens to be the oldest in the city, because of its well-curated selection of both interesting, independent films & quality blockbusters. After a recent revamp, this cinema is back and better than ever. We've never been more excited to sit quietly in the dark for hours on end.

Haarlemmerdijk 161
doors & ticket office open half an hour before the first film

THE MOVIES
1 JOKER
BLADE RUNNER
2 PORTRAIT DE LA JEUNE FILLE EN FEU
AMAZING GRACE
THE GOLDFINCH
DOWNTON ABBEY
LIGHT OF MY LIFE
3 MILES DAVIS: BIRTH OF THE COOL
ROH.
4 AIC: GAUGUIN IN TAHITI
DOLOR Y GLORIA
ONCE UPON A TIME ... IN HOLLYWOOD
RESTAURANT
TAVENU

GRACHTEN-GORDEL

Want to know our favourite stretch of canal in Grachtengordel?
Head to de Gouden Bocht at sunset. Thank us later.

GET TO KNOW GRACHTEN-GORDEL

If you're not Dutch, we'd bet you probably can't pronounce it, but that certainly should not keep you from visiting one of our very favourite neighbourhoods. Grachtengordel, or the Canal District, is a gorgeous area in the centre of Amsterdam, with the concentric semi-circles of the 17th-century canals forming its skeleton. The Singel, the Herengracht, the Keizersgracht and the Prinsengracht are always buzzing with life and brimming with history–the canal belt is actually a UNESCO World Heritage site! Pretty cool, no?

We'd say we end up either in or whizzing through Grachtengordel just about every day of the week. Long, sunny summer evenings are spent sipping a glass of Beaujolais with a plate of ravioli at Buffet van Odette, and early mornings are made infinitely more pleasant by a fresh espresso & banana bread from Back to Black and a quick trip to FlowerLovesMe, the dreamiest flower shop. Grachtengordel is truly the heart of Amsterdam.

Carmen Atiyah de Baets & Joris ter Meulen Swijtink

gloobles curators Grachtengordel

If we'd never met Carmen & Joris before, we easily could have found them intimidating. The pair are undeniably cool; everything they do seems effortless, unstudied. And, like Midas, whatever they touch somehow turns to gold—just look at their café-shop-guesthouse CARMEN. But despite all this cool, despite that enviable, untouchable vibe, Carmen & Joris are warm, relaxed and seriously down to earth.

"Even though we're in a relatively touristy part of the city, these places feel like they really belong to *Amsterdammers*."

Our story with Grachtengordel actually began a few generations ago. Joris's grandmother bought the two buildings where we live and house our guesthouse, shop and café back in the 80s. She spent decades living and working here on the Keizersgracht, so the neighbourhood has an especially nostalgic feel for Joris. When we moved into the place in 2018, we knew we wanted to create something that could be a hub for the neighbourhood. The previous tenants had noted just how much Grachtengordel had changed over the years – stalwarts of the Spiegelstraat had closed down, chains moved in – so we really wanted to make something that would last.

There are a few nice spots that are trying their best to maintain the character of the neighbourhood. There's this gallery down the street from us that focuses on Italian mid-century and classic Dutch art that we love. It's been there for years, and the owner is really adamant about staying. He's quite a character. And that's kind of what you see with a lot of these places that have been around for so long.

Another great neighbourhood place is Patisserie Holtkamp on the Vijzelgracht. They've been there since 1969, and the interior is a gorgeous example of the Amsterdam School. We love their traditional Dutch snacks, like their sausage roll and shrimp croquettes. Café de Wetering, the brown café on Weteringstraat, is another great spot that feels really local. Or Café Alto, which is this amazing jazz club that's just a few blocks away.

Even though we're in a relatively touristy part of the city, these places feel like they really belong to *Amsterdammers*.

Hayley Daen

editorial director of gloobles

South Carolina bred, UK educated and Netherlands enthused, Hayley has an insatiable hunger for travel and, of course, all things delicious. A traveller as seasoned as her cast iron skillet, Hayley always knows the best spots for a tasty bite or a cheeky glass. When she's not digging up killer hole-in-the-wall falafel spots in Beirut or trying (sometimes vainly!) to find inspiring exhibitions across the globe, she's busy crafting copy for gloobles as the Editorial Director.

"In general, Amsterdam has so much energy, but there's no area I find more charming or dynamic than the gorgeous canal ring."

Ever since I moved to the Netherlands back in the early, dreary days of 2016, I have been in love with Grachtengordel. In fact, though my parents had lived in both Oud-Zuid and the Museumkwartier in the past, I have never lived in another neighbourhood. Why do I love it? Let me count the ways.

In general, Amsterdam has so much energy, but there's no area I find more charming, more dynamic than the canal ring. The buildings are beautiful, there is no shortage of fantastic restaurants or cool shops, but it still has a little bit of grit, a little bit of mystery about it. It's not as subdued as Oud-Zuid. It's not as manic as Centrum. It's not as unpolished as Oud-West. To me, it's perfect.

I travel a lot (hey, I do work at gloobles, after all), but whenever I'm lucky enough to be in Amsterdam, I have a hard time peeling myself away from Grachtengordel. But really, why would I?

On bright, crisp Saturday mornings, I like to wake up early and hit the streets. Sure, it's tough to resist the siren call of my bed, but that of my neighbourhood is even sweeter. I weave my way along the leafy canals, keeping my eyes peeled for new & exciting things. I'll grab a milky oolong tea at Back to Black and pop into FlowerLovesMe on my way back to pick out a bouquet for the week.

If the cupboards are bare at home—which they often are come Saturday morning—then there's nothing better than a leisurely lunch on the terrace at Buffet van Odette. Because I'm always torn between the truffle cheese omelette & the ravioli, I always lure a friend out with me so we can go halfsies. The same (un)lucky friend is also likely to be dragged around the corner once we've finished, as there is no cosier bar in the world than Café de Wetering. I settle in at one of the tables nestled by the roaring fire and play cards with a *wijntje* or two. On very good days, the owner of De Wetering sweeps through the bar with a tray piled high with nuggets of cheese & nose-tinglingly strong mustard or slices of sausage & Saltines.

Come evening, when the wine has taken hold and a little stomach-lining is in order, I'll stumble over to Bambino for dinner. Small plates, often big flavours and, of course, excellent vibes. The ideal end to an ideal day on the canals.

Then, as I zip home on my bike, enchanted by my city, by my neighbourhood, a little tune starts running through my head. A steady beat. The unmistakable thump of a snare drum. The twang of guitar. Ahhhh. This must be the place.

Jetteke van Lexmond

gloobles curator Grachtengordel

Chic through and through, Jetteke is our north star when we're looking for elegant restaurants, great shops and cool places to hang or work. This mega creative fashion editor and co-founder of MoonSisters rules the roost from her home in Amsterdam. She loves shimmying through the canals with her family, running into friends, soaking up the beauty of the city and, of course, getting it all done. For us, missing a tip from Jetteke is a non-negotiable. It should be for you too.

"You can live quietly and under the radar if you want, but you also have all the charm of living in a village."

Grachtengordel is a neighbourhood that's really for the people who live here. Obviously, you get an occasional tourist, but in general, it feels like it belongs to the *Amsterdammers*. It's like a little village where everybody knows each other, but it still manages to feel calm and secluded.

On Mondays, there's an amazing market at beautiful Amstelveld (there's also a cosy antique market on the first Friday of every month during spring & summer) behind an old wooden church. All of the farmers from outside the city bring wonderful produce and plants and, of course, flowers. I love starting my week here, chatting to friends and picking up what I need for the week. Once I've secured my flowers, I usually head over to Maha+ for a coffee. They use raw milk from a farmer named MOMA, which not only makes the coffee incredibly delicious but also gives you all these great health benefits.

As the neighbourhood is always evolving, we also have excellent new local heroes like Cenc (from the team behind Balthazar's Keuken and Bar Parry). Wanne, the son of one of my favourite photographers whom I worked with for years at *Vogue* and *Glamour*, is in the kitchen, and he just makes the greatest seafood dishes. It's stylish and cosy and delicious. While it's not new–it's actually been around for decades–Buffet van Odette is another local hero. Odette and her daughter Lisa, the owners, churn out wonderful farm-to-table food. Everyone from the neighbourhood congregates here, so it's a fun mix of famous creative people and locals.

Somehow, the Utrechtsestraat became this brilliant, buzzing street with three Michelin-starred restaurants. Bistro de la Mer is one of our favourites, but we're also big fans of more relaxed spots like CARMEN and more elevated places like the Waldorf Astoria (great for high tea!).

If you're looking for something to do other than eat, I highly recommend wandering down the Nieuwe Spiegelstraat to check out some of the antique shops. Kramer Kunst & Antiek is a great shop that sells the silver trinkets and the most beautiful *Delfts Blauw* ceramics–just ask the staff about the history of these pots! When I need to do some work, I like popping into Fosbury & Sons; you can grab a day pass if you're not a member. And, when I want to work out, I am a big fan of Core40. You can buy a credit for just one Pilates class or five or ten, and it's ideal for clearing your head.

This part of the canals is the perfect picture of real Amsterdam life. You can live quietly and under the radar if you want, but you also have all the charm of living in a village. When you're in Grachtengordel, you're always going to run into a friend or two.

Stephanie van Rappard

CEO & Founder of gloobles

Ever since she was little, Stephanie has been travelling. Near, far, but always with a focus on finding culture. Over the years, Stephanie laid down roots in several cosmopolitan cities—New York, London & Paris—but these days she's happy to be back in her very own city, Amsterdam. When she is not honing, growing & shaping gloobles around the clock, she leads several charitable projects at home and abroad. Want to know her favourite destination or cause? That's like picking a favourite child for Stephanie.

"Once I started my family, I knew there was nowhere else we'd want to live."

I spent most of my childhood running around quiet, residential Oud-Zuid. When I moved back to Amsterdam after my studies over fifteen years ago, however, I knew that I absolutely had to live near the magical canals. I've lived in many cool, bustling places, but the canals that criss-cross Amsterdam make it my very favourite city on the planet.

After doing some field research exploring neighbourhoods, I fell in love with an oft-overlooked part of Grachtengordel, the *gezellige* Weteringbuurt. I love that it's so very close to buzzing Centrum and peaceful Oud-Zuid and right in the middle of Grachtengordel. Weteringbuurt is a hidden village within the Dutch capital. Everyone knows each other, and few tourists have really discovered it. It's the perfect place to live if you have kids, so once my three boys, Beer, Ties & Splinter, came along, I knew I was here to stay.

When I wake up and look outside my window, I see a beautiful, leafy garden; I couldn't imagine a better view. I love going for a morning run in the Vondelpark or heading to a Pilates class at Bodyvita - Kerkstraat just around the corner. When I have a day off, I can't resist spending it exploring the neighbourhood with my family.

On a sunny day, we walk along the canals and get coffee & banana bread (the best in town) at Back to Black - Weteringstraat. Once we're full & happy, we pop into Museum van Loon for some history & magnificent architecture. Afterwards, we walk to *Amstelveldje*, Amsterdam's cutest square. Everyone from our neighbourhood who has children gathers there as soon as the weather is nice. The newly opened Café Marcella is a great place to catch up with friends over coffee & croissants or *biertjes* & *bitterballen* while the kids tumble about the square.

If we haven't run out of steam yet, we'll meet with friends (& their children) for drinks at café twee prinsen, which has a lovely, sunny terrace. It can be quite dangerous though, as they've got a terrific selection of incredible, natural wines. Somehow, one glass of wine often transforms into a bottle or two. I love the unpretentious vibe & the simple Dutch décor. We always love to try new places for dinner, but if we are feeling lazy, we simply walk to Zoldering for relaxed Michelin-star food and affordable, quality wines.

As you probably can see, Grachtengordel has everything you could want, neatly contained in one lovely, stunning neighbourhood. It's no wonder I love it so.

GRACHTENGORDEL

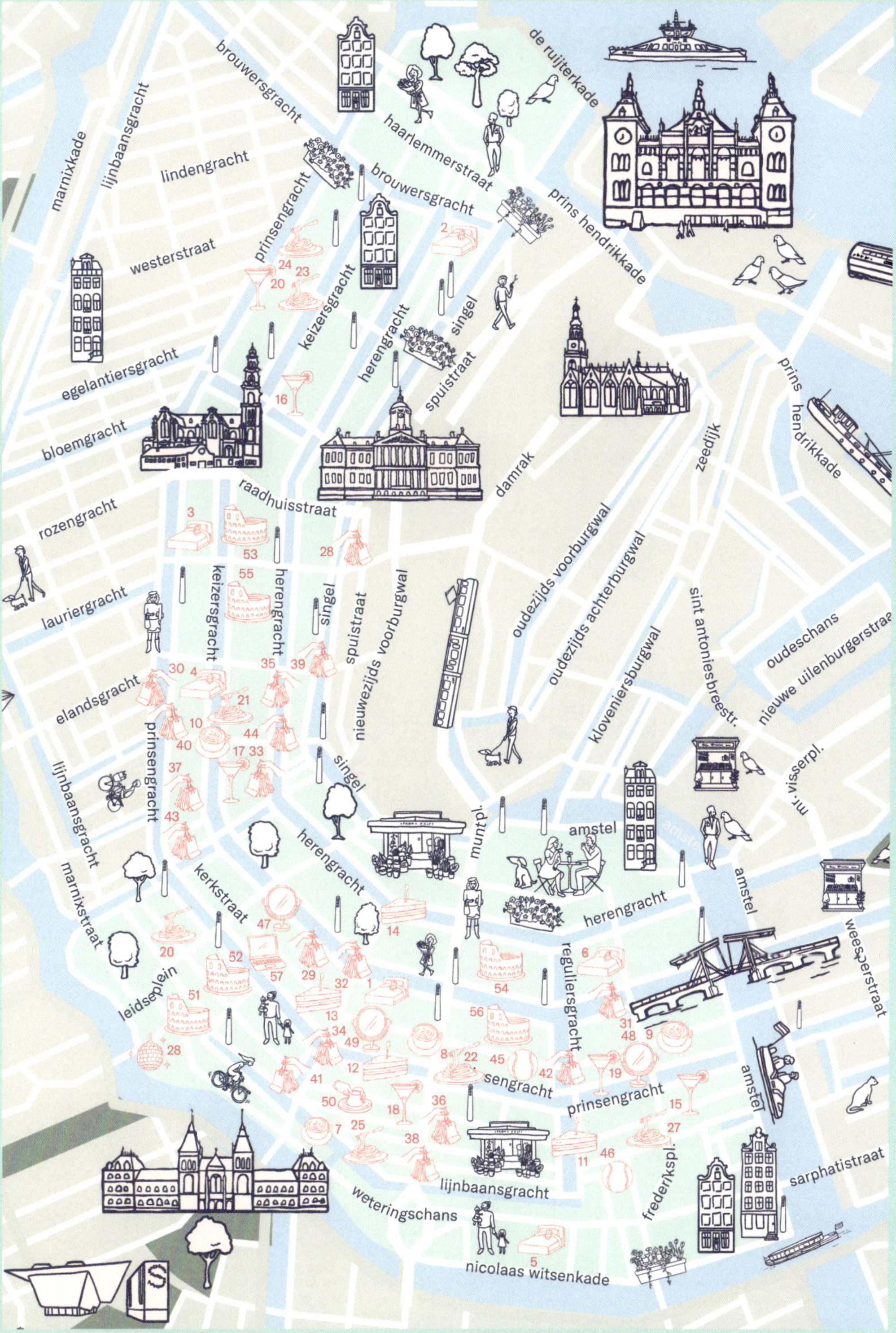
de ruijterkade
brouwersgracht
haarlemmerstraat
prins hendrikkade
marnixkade
lijnbaansgracht
lindengracht
prinsengracht
westerstraat
keizersgracht
herengracht
singel
spuistraat
egelantiersgracht
bloemgracht
raadhuisstraat
damrak
zeedijk
rozengracht
lauriergracht
nieuwezijds voorburgwal
oudezijds voorburgwal
oudezijds achterburgwal
kloveniersburgwal
sint antoniesbreestr.
oudeschans
nieuwe uilenburgerstraat
elandsgracht
mr. visserpl.
muntpl.
amstel
kerkstraat
marnixstraat
leidseplein
reguliersgracht
weesperstraat
prinsengracht
frederikspl.
sarphatistraat
lijnbaansgracht
weteringschans
nicolaas witsenkade

GRACHTENGORDEL

get sleepy

sleep. breakfast. coffee. lunch. drinks. takeout. shop.

CARMEN

Every It-Girl and every It-Boy in Amsterdam knows that THE place to be is CARMEN. Run by Carmen Atiyah de Baets and her husband Joris, this guesthouse-kitchen-shop is a delightful mishmash bursting with style. Book a room or simply peruse the racks. CARMEN is a feast for each and every sense.

Keizersgracht 600
shop: Monday 11am-6pm
& Thursday-Sunday 11am-6pm
kitchen: Monday 9.30am-3.30pm
& Thursday-Sunday 9.30am-3.30pm

sleep.

Herengracht 21

This refreshing, contemporary bed & breakfast is tucked away in an incredible 17th-century canal house on the Herengracht. The whole b&b is dotted with works created by local artists. Wander out to the sunny terrace to enjoy their delicious complimentary breakfast while you try to puzzle out the morning's news in *Het Parool*. If you get more than a few words, colour us impressed.

Herengracht 21
+31 20 625 6305

sleep. drinks.

Pulitzer

This sophisticated, privately-owned boutique hotel is spread across 25 gorgeously restored 17th- & 18th-century canal houses. Its central location in the heart of the buzzing *De Negen Straatjes* makes it an ideal jumping off point for a day of culture or shopping. We can't resist an afternoon drink in the garden courtyard and adore booking the hotel's boat for a cruise around the canals.

Prinsengracht 323
+31 20 523 5235

sleep. drinks. dinner.

The Dylan

This truly luxurious hotel might just be our top pick in Amsterdam when we feel like treating ourselves. The hotel is spread between two stunning historic canal houses with jaw-dropping original interior details. Ask for one of the loft rooms with beautiful exposed beams, then book a seat at their secret 6-seater restaurant até. When it's chilly, settle in for a glass of wine in front of the fireplace and refuse to move.

Keizersgracht 384
+31 20 530 2010

sleep.

Villa Nicola

Itching to feel like a real local and not your run of the mill tourist checking in at a big, anonymous hotel? Book one of two suites at the intimate, charming Villa Nicola. The whole place oozes style & grandeur, which is a perfect complement to the lovely, leafy part of De Pijp it's tucked away in. Breakfast in bed is taken up a notch here, as the owner personally whips up breakfast for his guests whenever hunger strikes.

Nicolaas Witsenkade 21
+31 61 591 5410

sleep. coffee. drinks. beauty.

Waldorf Astoria

Let's be honest. You know you pretty much can't go wrong when you're staying at a Waldorf, and this stunning hotel spanning 6 monumental 17th-century canal palaces on the 'Gentleman's Canal' is no different. With an incredible Guerlain spa, this hotel is the ideal place to take a breath & relax, away from the bustling crowds of the city.

Herengracht 542-556
+31 20 718 4600

get coffee

breakfast. coffee. takeout.

Back to Black – Wetering

Both the espresso & filter coffee (roasted in-house) options change on a regular basis, so you'll always have something fresh & exciting to drink when you're here. They also serve up a wonderful range of sweet & savoury snacks, so it's easy to spend an afternoon here nibbling on something delicious while you sip top-notch espresso after top-notch espresso.

Weteringstraat 48
Monday-Friday 8am-6pm & Saturday-Sunday 9am-6pm
+31 20 771 8364

coffee. takeout. shop.

Maha & Maha+

In a city where the word 'heels' raises eyebrows, having chic sneaks and cute pieces that make zipping around on your bike a breeze is an absolute must. Hunt for feminine yet funky streetwear at Maha before popping over to their café next door for a perfectly foamed latte. Great coffee and stylish clothes? A combination we never knew we needed.

Vijzelstraat 103h & 129
Maha+: Monday-Friday 8.30am-4.30pm
& Saturday-Sunday 10am-5pm
Maha: Monday 1-6pm & Tuesday-Saturday 10.30am-6pm
& Sunday 1-6pm
+31 20 221 7886

coffee. takeout.

Screaming Beans – Utrechtsestraat

With their own mini empire in Amsterdam, Screaming Beans is an excellent place to refuel and recharge. The baristas here really know their stuff, so if you're stuck on what to order, they'll guide you with care and expertise. We've set up a standing order of their beans so we can make coffee that's almost as good when we're at home.

Utrechtsestraat 75
Monday-Friday 8am-5pm & Saturday-Sunday 9am-6pm

get lunch

lunch. dinner.

Bouchon du Centre

You'll forget all about the bicycles whizzing by and the canals snaking through the city when you sit down at Bouchon du Centre for lunch. "Amsterdam, who?" you'll ask. This rustic Lyonnaise bistro is warm & welcoming, with a menu brimming with bouchon staples like *andouillette*, *boudin noir* & *oeufs en meurette*. Don't forget to order a bottle of Beaujolais!

Falckstraat 3
Wednesday-Saturday 12-4pm
+31 20 330 1128

lunch. drinks. dinner.

Buffet van Odette

Though we're suggesting you come here for lunch, you pretty much can't go wrong at Buffet van Odette, no matter the time of day. The space is beautiful & intimate, with a lovely little terrace outside. The truffle cheese omelette & sticky toffee cake are the stuff of legends here in Amsterdam. Settle in for a delicious lunch & a fantastic glass of wine and while away the afternoon.

Prinsengracht 598
Wednesday-Saturday 12-3pm, 5.30-11pm
+31 20 423 6034

coffee. lunch. takeout. shop.

ZERO ZERO – Spiegelstraat

Finally! An insanely good sandwich spot in the centre of town. We feel as if we've been waiting for Zero Zero to open for the last decade. Luckily, it was worth the wait. Run by an Italian pizza chef, Zero Zero serves up killer combinations like *mortadella* and *stracciatella* on their homemade *schiacciata* (a flatbread similar to focaccia).

Nieuwe Spiegelstraat 3A
Monday-Friday 8am-5pm
& Saturday-Sunday 9am-5pm
+31 20 244 6877

get drinks

drinks.

Bar Babar

It turns out that the ever-dapper Babar is just as charming now that we're adults as he was when we were children. Bathed in warm light and rich jewel tones, this easy little bar is perfect for dates. Or for finding a date for next week! Come by for a few glasses of wine, a dish of olives and a nice people-watching session.

Utrechtsestraat 135
Tuesday- Thursday 5pm-1am & Friday 4pm-1am & Saturday 3pm-1am

drinks. dancing.

Café Brandon

Want to escape from throngs of (other) tourists? Café Brandon is quintessentially Amsterdam. Quirky décor. Quirkier bartenders. And an occasional rogue smoker spotted inside. If you're after something slick and sleek, look elsewhere. But if you want something authentic, Brandon's got your name written all over it.

Keizersgracht 157
Monday-Wednesday 3pm-1am & Thusday 3pm-3am
& Friday 12pm-3am & Saturday-Sunday 12pm-1am

coffee. drinks.

Café de Pels

Tucked away in the middle of *De Negen Straatjes* is Café de Pels. It may look unassuming & unexciting at first glance, but we implore you to give it a chance. It's the dreamiest respite from a day of brisk shopping and the ideal place to spend a rainy afternoon – they've got a killer selection of national & international newspapers. Order a *biertje* or two, and maybe a toastie if you're feeling a bit peckish, and enjoy some of the best people watching around.

Huidenstraat 25
Monday-Thursday 9-1am & Friday-Saturday 9-2am
& Sunday 9-1am
+31 20 622 9037

drinks.

Café de Wetering

"This is, hands down, the absolute best bar in the world."

— Hayley

It's pretty tough to pick favourites in our wonderful city, but, if pressed, we might go out on a limb and say that Café de Wetering is our very favourite bar in Amsterdam. It's the true definition of *gezellig*. There's a roaring fireplace upstairs & plenty of games to keep you entertained if the beers aren't quite doing it.

Weteringstraat 37
Monday-Thursday 4pm-1am & Friday 4pm-2am
& Saturday 3pm-2am & Sunday 3-10pm
+31 20 622 9676

coffee. drinks.

Café Marcella

Did we *need* another cutesy bar on the canals? Not really, we thought. But after visiting Café Marcella, we've changed our tune. Big time. This charming, red-awninged café on the Prinsengracht is a lovely spot for a long, languorous breakfast with the paper in tow as it is for a buoyant, booze-filled afternoon with friends on the weekend. They've scored serious bonus points for their elevated *borrelhapjes*.

Amstelveld 21
Monday-Thursday 9am-12am & Friday-Saturday 9am-2am & Sunday 9-12am
+31 20 235 8730

coffee. lunch. drinks. dinner.

café twee prinsen

As evidenced by café binnenvisser, bakkerij louf and cornerstore, Bob Nagel and Maarten Bloem know a thing or two about building out true hotspots. café twee prinsen, their fourth outpost, is no different. This cosy spot is chill as chill can be. Delicious wines pair seamlessly with a concise menu of small bites.

Prinsenstraat 27
Monday-Thursday 2pm-12am & Friday 2pm-1am
& Saturday 12pm-1am & Sunday 1pm-12am

get dinner

dinner.

até

Whew! Pricey, yes. But worth it? Absolutely. Absolutely. até is a whirlwind from start to finish. This elegant omakase simply has to be one of the best in Amsterdam. With just six seats in the restaurant, até is a difficult reservation to snag. Save your pennies and stalk the reservations line. You're in for a treat.

Keizersgracht 384
Wednesday-Saturday 7-10pm
+31 20 530 2010

dinner.

Bar Gui

To Brittany and beyond! Chef Guillaume de Beer (you might remember him from Breda back in the day) takes you on a journey to this beautiful corner of France—all from the comfort of this familiar corner on the Prinsengracht. It's certainly a spot for a splurge, so squirrel away those pennies and snag a reservation for a special occasion.

Prinsengracht 955
Monday-Thursday 6pm-12am & Friday-Sunday 12pm-12am
+31 63 950 7459

lunch. drinks. dinner.

Café de Klepel

This wildly popular table d'hôte is buzzy for a reason. The laid-back French food is delicious—we like to order the weekly four-course menu and settle in for a long, lovely evening. You can't order à la carte, but trust us, you won't miss it. If the weather is nice, ask for a table outside and be sure to sufficiently probe the host to discover the very best wine.

Prinsenstraat 22
Monday-Thursday 5pm-12am & Friday-Sunday 3pm-12am
+31 20 623 8244

lunch. drinks. dinner.

Kikkie van de Prinsensluis

Our dream is to be considered 'regulars' at all of our favourite hotspots in town, and next on our hitlist is none other than Kikkie van de Prinsensluis. The vibe of a brown bar with a menu and wine list to rival any top bar à vins in Paris, this supremely inviting spot on a quiet corner in De Jordaan is our idea of heaven. Whatever you do, order the burger.

Corner of Prinsenstraat & Prinsengracht
Monday-Thursday 12pm-1am & Friday 12pm-2am
& Saturday 11-2am & Sunday 12-10pm
+31 20 224 6022

lunch. dinner.

Restaurant Watergang

Taking over a space from a beloved restaurant can be tricky, as the old ardent supporters are likely to lament the changeover. Miraculously, Restaurant Watergang has managed to fill the very big shoes of La Cacerola. The table d'hôte menu at Restaurant Watergang changes monthly and focuses on inventive takes on hearty comfort food classics. The service is friendly & attentive without being overbearing, so it's a great spot for a long, tranquil dinner.

Weteringstraat 41
Wednesday-Thursday 6pm-12am
& Friday-Sunday 12.30-4.30pm, 6pm-12am
+31 63 867 8170

dinner.

Sushi Hanabi

In Japan, precision and quality reign supreme. The team at Sushi Hanabi have brought that ethos of excellence to their teeny-tiny omakase spot on the Leidseplein. Normally a…shall we say… unglamourous area, this square in the centre of Amsterdam might just be on the up-and-up thanks to the stellar sushi and yakitori at this 10-seat spot.

Leidseplein 10
Tuesday-Saturday 5-11pm
+31 20 730 1332

dinner. shop.

Zoldering & Lof

Honestly, we don't know what keeps us coming back to Zoldering more: the perfectly precise food or the insane wine list. Despite the fact that Zoldering has secured its very own Michelin star, the restaurant is intimate and unpretentious. The perfect combination if you ask us. Ensure you book promptly, as spots fill up quickly. If you fall in love with a bottle during dinner, hop by Lof, their wine shop on the Haarlemmerdijk, to stock your shelves.

Utrechtsestraat 141h, Haarlemmerdijk 87
Zoldering: Monday-Saturday 5.30-10pm
Lof: Tuesday-Friday 11am-7pm & Saturday 10am-6pm
+31 20 765 1212

get groovy

dancing. culture.

Paradiso

Though many people know Amsterdam for its festivals, particularly Dekmantel & ADE, it's also home to an incredible, historic music venue whose fame stretches well beyond the Dutch borders. Paradiso also serves as a cool cultural centre, so you should check their website to find out what exciting things are going on in the near future. Get ready to get groovy.

Weteringschans 6-8
opening hours vary, so check the website
+31 20 626 4521

get shopping

shop.

A.P Bloem

One of the things the Netherlands is best known for is flowers; if you've ever visited Keukenhof, you'll understand why. You can get the most jaw-dropping arrangements no matter where you are in Amsterdam, but one of the best places to source them is A.P Bloem. The incredibly friendly staff will help you assemble a gorgeous arrangement.

Kerkstraat 151a
Tuesday-Saturday 9am-5pm
+31 20 223 1616

A·P Bloem

shop.

Anouk Beerents

Mirror, mirror on the wall, who's the fairest of them all? Well, when it comes to shops in Amsterdam, the top billing most certainly goes to Anouk Beerents. This stunning antique store is worth a visit, if only to stare lovingly into the intricately carved gold mirrors flanking the walls. Anouk is a master of mirrors, so if you are in the market, she can help guide you to ensure you pick the perfect piece.

Prinsengracht 467bg
by appointment only
+31 20 622 8598

coffee. shop.

Concerto

These days, most of us are used to streaming music on Spotify or SoundCloud, but we think there's something to be said for good old-fashioned records & CDs. Concerto is an amazing place to browse or pick up any form or style of music you could dream of. Order an espresso at the bar and get carried away in the wild selection of music & videos.

Utrechtsestraat 54-60
Monday 12-6pm & Tuesday-Saturday 10am-6pm
& Sunday 12-6pm
+31 20 261 2610

shop.

FlowerLovesMe

In a country known far & wide for its blooms, it can start to feel like floral overload. But just because wonderful florists are nearly a dime a dozen here doesn't mean that there aren't a few truly unique places to pick up a bouquet or a few plants for the house. With its distinctive style & diminutive space, FlowerLovesMe is a definite standout.

Nieuwe Spiegelstraat 28
Tuesday-Saturday 9am-6.30pm & Sunday 11am-6.30pm
+31 64 870 9023

shop.

Gray Label

Is there anything cuter than a well dressed kid? Well, if there is, we can't think of it. For the chic little minimalist in your life, you absolutely must go to Gray Label. This adorable shop sells well-crafted, timeless clothing made from organic fabrics that will have you wishing you could shrink an inch or five. You'll find it hard not to say, "Are you sure that doesn't come in my size?"

Huidenstraat 17
Monday 12-6pm & Tuesday-Saturday 11am-6pm
& Sunday 12-5pm
+31 20 786 9916

"Leonore van der Waals & her mother, Inez Stodel, know everything about the history of jewellery. Their store is like a museum."

— Judith

shop.

Inez Stodel

Not all that glitters is gold, but there sure is a heck of a lot that glitters here at Inez Stodel. This wonderful shop sells a wide selection of rare & wearable antique jewellery from their shop on the Nieuwe Spiegelstraat. Expect jewels from grand houses like Van Cleef & Arpels, Boucheron and Cartier, ranging from antiquity to the 1970s.

Nieuwe Spiegelstraat 65
Opening hours: By appointment
+31 20 623 2942

shop.

Love Stories

Sometimes you want something seriously slinky, but sometimes you just want gorgeously feminine, perfectly candy-coloured pyjamas and lingerie. In those moments, there's only one place to go: Love Stories. This true Amsterdam brand is the go-to for all things underthings. Plus bathing suits and accessories and jewellery and more.

Herengracht 298
Monday-Saturday 11am-6pm & Sunday 12-5pm
+31 20 210 3034

shop.

Patisserie Holtkamp

This family-owned pastry shop is worth a visit for the interior design alone. That being said, their pastries are pretty damn good too. They have a fantastic selection of French & Dutch patisserie, but their (typically Dutch) *kroketten* are the most popular with local *Amsterdammers*. You've got to do as the locals do.

Vijzelgracht 15
Monday-Friday 8.30am-6pm & Saturday 8.30am-5pm
+31 20 624 8757

shop.

Prinsheerlijk Antiek

The itch to return to Prinsheerlijk Antiek on a weekly basis is quite strong, but often it's well rewarded too, as Harald and the team fill the rooms of the shop with new treasures regularly. Prinsheerlijk Antiek is great for uncovering tiny treasures & trinkets and beautiful pieces of furniture, too.

Prinsengracht 579
Monday 11am-6pm & Wednesday-Saturday 11am-6pm
& Sunday 2-6pm
+31 20 638 6623

takeout. shop.

Proper. Indofood

There's a long, storied (and undeniably difficult) relationship between Indonesia and the Netherlands, and you can find a solid showing of great Indonesian restaurants here in Amsterdam as a result. In our opinion, one of them stands far above the rest: Proper. Indofood. If we could, we'd probably get takeaway from this Vijzelgracht hotspot every week. We only wish we could dine-in here!

Vijzelgracht 20
Tuesday-Sunday 3:30-8:30pm
+31 64 551 6274

shop.

Rika Studios

If you've noticed hordes of cool-girls winding their way through the city and wondered where they picked up that chic jumper or incredible bracelet, you'd better make your way to Rika Studios. Stop into the supremely stylish shop and rifle through racks of luxurious women's clothing. They also stock jewellery by Delfina Delletrez & Le Labo products.

Oude Spiegelstraat 12
Monday 12-6pm & Tuesday-Saturday 11am-6pm
& Sunday 1-5pm
+31 62 758 9099

shop.

Tamago

There's vintage clothing, and then there's *vintage clothing*. And if you're after the serious stuff – think classic Missoni, covetable Céline and old school Prada – Tamago is the place to be. If you're looking to earn a little before you spend a little, Tamago is ideal, as they consign pristine designer clothes, doing all the work for you. Dream!

Spiegelgracht 13
Thursday-Saturday 11am-6pm
+31 20 626 6054

shop.

The Archive Store

This warm, soothing shop specialises in lovely, unique (& sustainable) pieces for little ones. If you're on the hunt for a gift for your friend's new-born or toddler, this is the ideal shop for you. Even if you're more interested in decorating a nursery than shopping for knick-knacks, The Archive Store has you covered. We especially adore the Sebra cot they stock.

Reguliersgracht 70
Tuesday 11am-5pm & Thursday-Saturday 11am-5pm
+31 61 504 0109

shop.

The Frozen Fountain

We obviously love discovering new places (it's part of what makes our job fun!), but we enjoy rediscovering beloved spots nearly as much. If not more! The Frozen Fountain has been championing innovative Dutch design for decades; nearly 40 years later, they're just as relevant. Pick up a few beautiful pieces or simply browse the shop for the ultimate in home inspiration.

Prinsengracht 645
Tuesday-Saturday 10am-6pm
+31 20 622 9375

shop.

Velour

Not all of the shops in *De Negen Straatjes* are worth a visit, but if you're into funky, contemporary designers, Velour certainly is. The shop is small with a tightly edited collection of pieces from brands like Nanushka, Low Classic, Róhe and NN07. Keep an eye out for their semi-regular sales, as you can score some seriously good deals.

Huidenstraat 14
Monday 12-7pm & Tuesday-Friday 11am-7pm
& Saturday-Sunday 11am-6pm
+31 20 210 0163

get active

activity.

Soda Bodyfit

With all the eating & drinking you're likely doing when you're in Amsterdam, we wouldn't blame you if you wanted to work up a little sweat. Sometimes, we love participating in group classes where we can play off of the energy of others. Other times, we prefer to get our heart rates going in a more intimate setting. That's when we head to Soda Bodyfit, a personal training studio run by celebrity trainer Radmilo Soda.

Falckstraat 11
Monday-Friday 7am-10pm & Saturday-Sunday 9am-5pm
+31 20 846 1076

get beautiful

beauty.

Assort International Hair Salon

For one reason or another – and we really couldn't say why to be honest, Amsterdam is riddled with hair salons. While we're sure you could pop into any one of them and get a decent haircut, Assort International Hair Salon is the place we go to time & time again when we want to look truly fabulous. All of the stylists are fantastic.

Kerkstraat 99a
Monday-Sunday 10am-7pm
+31 20 846 7746

beauty.

Pure Wellness

Biking around all the time often leaves us crumpled, crunched and with a crick or two in our necks. To remedy the situation, we fold back up on our bicycles and find our way over to Pure Wellness. Martha and her team at the diminutive spa work serious magic. It's by far and away our favourite place to work out those knots in town.

Prinsengracht 809
Monday-Friday 11am-8pm & Saturday 10am-5pm
+31 61 504 0109

get creative

creativity.

The Mallow Garden

A Waldorf mini community, The Mallow Garden is a sweet weekly play group in the heart of Amsterdam's Weteringbuurt. Beyond the classic visits, The Mallow Garden organizes fun, engaging sessions on things like crafts and kombucha. Holistic creativity is central to The Mallow Garden's ethos, so your wee'uns will love learning from the get-go.

Weteringstraat 34
check their website for current and upcoming sessions.
+31 65 336 1603

get cultured

drinks. dancing. culture.

De Balie

When we realised we'd left this Amsterdam icon out of the first and second edition of the book, we were shocked! This wonderful cultural centre has a meticulous program of debates, theatre and talks with a focus on social and political subjects. Grab a coffee in the in-house café afterward for a debrief with new and old friends.

Kleine-Gartmanplantsoen 10
Monday-Thursday 10am-11pm & Friday-Saturday 10am-1am & Sunday 10am-11pm
+31 20 553 5100

culture.

De Uitkijk

This has to be just about the cutest cinema we've ever seen. De Uitkijk is an iconic 1920s arthouse theatre with just one screen. But that one screen? Well, it shows some of the best films out there, from cult classics like Midnight Cowboy to more recent independent movies. There's no popcorn here, so we like to sneak in our own snacks to nibble on with a glass of the house red.

Prinsengracht 452
see show times
+31 20 223 2416

shop. culture.

Eddy Varekemp

Grand museums abound here in Amsterdam. Broad, sweeping galleries, too. We love them, sure. But we also love things on a slightly smaller scale. Eddy Varekamp is a charming little gallery that features the ceramics, paintings and stencil prints crafted by the gallery's namesake. They don't ship, so you'd better carve out a few moments to pick up a treasure in person.

Hartenstraat 30
Thursday-Sunday 1-5pm

culture.

Foam

Every hipster in Amsterdam (and believe us there are many) has been to Foam once or twice in their day. This cool, contemporary museum focuses on photography & photography alone. They've an ever-changing roster of impressive exhibitions from photography icons to up-and-coming talent. Once you've sauntered through the museum, hit the gift shop. You can never have too many coffee table books & posters.

Keizersgracht 609
Monday-Wednesday 10am-6pm & Thursday-Friday 10am-9pm
& Saturday-Sunday 10am-6pm
+31 20 551 6500

ANNO
1861.
MUSEUM FODOR
609
foam
611

culture.

GRIMM Gallery

If we're honest, we'd say that Amsterdam is far better known for its museums than for its galleries. With that said, there are a few galleries that never fail to impress us with their well-curated exhibitions. One such spot is GRIMM Gallery. We adore its sleek, minimalist interiors & its terrific collection of contemporary art. Pop into their gallery on the Keizersgracht to take in the latest exhibitions.

Keizersgracht 241
Tuesday-Saturday 11am-6pm
+31 20 675 2465

coffee. culture.

Museum van Loon

Museum van Loon is a magnificent canal house belonging to the Amsterdam regent family van Loon, co-founders of the Dutch East-India Company. These days, the house is open to the public; it's a wonderful window into how the upper ecehlons of Dutch society once lived. Take an exceptional guided tour to get a glimpse of the history of the van Loon family.

Keizersgracht 672
Monday-Sunday 10am-5pm
+31 20 624 5255

get to work

coffee. lunch. work.

Fosbury & Sons

If you find yourself in need of an inspiring place to work for the day, hunker down at Fosbury & Sons (you can buy a day pass if you aren't a member). While you're there, grab a bite at their in-house restaurant. The space is gorgeously outfitted; there are even striking mirrors designed by our friend Sabine Marcelis hanging on the walls.

Prinsengracht 769
Monday-Friday 8am-6pm
+31 20 787 1313

NOORD

Noord feels like no other part of Amsterdam,
and that's what we love about it.

GET TO KNOW NOORD

Ah, the great, undiscovered north of Amsterdam. Well, not totally unexplored these days, but we'd venture a guess that most people coming to Amsterdam for a quick visit have never had the pleasure of exploring this hip, incredible area. Separated from the rest of Amsterdam by the IJ, Noord has a totally different vibe to the other areas we tend to hang out in. This up-and-coming neighbourhood is a thriving hub of culture & activity, and we're spending more & more time here every year.

Once you've made it over on the ferry (you can totally take your bike!), you'll immediately breathe a sigh of relief. Noord is open, airy and very, very green. There's so much space that you'll almost forget the hustle & bustle of the other side. Carve out a day in your schedule to soak up all Noord has to offer, from buzzy cafés to leafy parks & impressive museums.

Stephanie Schuitemaker & Maurits de Boer

gloobles curators Noord

Creativity is just one of the red threads that bind Stephanie and Maurits together. This powerhouse couple, founders of ZELT (a studio that designs and builds textile structures and spaces) and Sustainder (an innovator in smart lighting for public spaces) respectively, are as well-versed in the wonders of their home city Amsterdam as they are in great Norwegian hiking spots, charming French farmhouses, *gemütlich* Alpine après-ski and inspiring contemporary design spaces. While they're true experts in all things caffeinated, artsy or leavened, we find ourselves seeking their advice no matter what we're on the hunt for.

"Taking the ferry feels like a breath of fresh air, as you take in the seasons & connect to the water."

Noord has been our home in Amsterdam for the last ten years, and we've seen it develop into the vibrant, creative hotspot it is today in an amazing way! For us, it captures the more playful & raw aspects of the city that we both love.

With the ferry going 24/7, Noord is just three minutes away from Centraal Station. Taking the ferry feels like a breath of fresh air, as you take in the seasons & connect to the water. Because of Noord's openness, some incredible sustainable projects have emerged. The sustainable floating village Schoonschip is definitely worth a visit for those interested in architecture & design. De Ceuvel is at its helm; it's an inspirational place that serves organic & locally grown food & drinks. It was one of the first places to combine sustainability & innovation in a fun, cool way at an old shipyard. We're thrilled to have one of Amsterdam's best swim spots right in our backyard, but unfortunately, 2023 will be the last year they're operational because of licensing.

Kometen Brood Café is the best spot to start your day, whether you're looking for a relaxed work environment during the week or a more vibrant atmosphere on the weekend. We love to kick off our weekends with cheese at KEF, an incredible cheese shop with a fun, knowledgeable team and its own tasting café, and wine from Chateau Karlito. Chateau Karlito does it all from wine to coffee to jazz with an incredible sound system.

For dinner, we love to go to cornerstore; it has a relaxed atmosphere and exceptional food. The new kid on the block, Café Restaurant Metro, is a delight for lunch and dinner. On summer days, the whole facade opens up; its huge terrace with sun-shading by ZELT.Studio is the place to be! The best pizza is definitely at Europizza, and the party continues next door at Bar Benelux. When we want something fancier, we treat ourselves to Café Modern, but dinner and a movie at FC Hyena is also wonderful.

klapozenweg
ridderspoorweg
distelweg
grasweg
asterweg
klapozenweg
kamperfoelieweg
hagedoorweg
johan van hasseltweg
IJ-tunnel
meeuwenlaan
noordwal
nieuwe leeuwarderweg
waddenweg
nieuwendammerdijk
zamenhofstraat
javakade
piet heinkade
prins
hendrikkade
damrak
oudezijds voorburgwal
kattenburgerstraat
wittenburgergracht
valkenburgerstraat
plantage middenlaan
weesperstraat
1
2
3
4
5
6
7
8
9
10
11
12
13
14
15

NOORD

get breakfast

breakfast. coffee. lunch. takeout. shop.

Kometen Brood

Yet another fantastic bakery in Noord, and we are definitely not complaining. Kometen Brood is a warm, inviting bakery and café on Ms. van Riemsdijkweg that knocks sourdough in all iterations – wheat, spelt, seeded – out of the park. They've got a nice, concise menu of salads, sandwiches and wines too, so it's also great for lunch or an afternoon snack.

Ms. van Riemsdijkweg 2
Monday-Friday 8am-4pm & Saturday-Sunday 8am-6pm

get lunch

breakfast. lunch. dinner. takeout.

Kebec Corner

When lunchtime rolls around, odds are we're craving one thing & one thing only: pizza. That's when we throw caution to the wind (and any plans for healthfulness we'd considered out the window) & head to Kebec. The pizza wizards at Kebec whip up the most craveable, focaccia-style pizza around. But if you want something a little more portable, they also make fantastic sandwiches.

tt. Melaniaweg 12
Wednesday-Thursday 9am-3pm & Friday 9am-8pm
& Saturday 4-8pm
+31 64 648 3643

get drinks

drinks.

Café 't Sluisje

With the laid-back, extra *gezellig* vibe that characterises Noord, it should come as no surprise that one of the best, most chilled brown cafés is smack dab in the middle. Café 't Sluisje is an old school pub where Noord locals have gone for over 100 years to fill up on *bitterballen* & a *biertje* or two. It's the perfect pit stop when exploring Noord by bike.

Nieuwendammerdijk 297
Monday 11am-11pm & Tuesday-Thursday 11-12am
& Friday-Saturday 11-1am & Sunday 11-12am
+31 20 636 1712

get dinner

lunch. drinks. dinner.

Bacalar

It's about damn time that Amsterdam got another spot to have top-notch Mexican food. We think it is more than worth the trek across the IJ to indulge in some killer tacos in a stunning converted industrial garage, so long as we get an ice-cold drink as soon as we step inside. Don't expect Tex-Mex standbys because Bacalar is the real deal.

Chrysantenstraat 4
Thursday 5.30-10pm & Friday 6-10pm
& Saturday-Sunday 12-10pm

breakfast. coffee. lunch. drinks. dinner.

Café Restaurant Metro

Was Noord actually missing another cool, seriously delicious restaurant? Not really. But do we welcome one? Well, when it's of as high a calibre as Café Restaurant Metro, we'll usher one in with gusto and tell all our friends about it. Smart modern European dishes in a gorge setting make for an ideal spot for breakfast, lunch or dinner.

Asterweg 22
Monday 10am-5pm & Tuesday-Thursday 10am-11pm
& Friday-Saturday 10am-1am & Sunday 10am-11pm
+31 65 336 1784

lunch. drinks. dinner.

Coba

Amsterdam is many wonderful things, but a hotspot for good Mexican food it was not. Until now, that is. Coba is an achingly cool restaurant serving a short & sweet menu of tacos, quesadillas & tostadas. If your thirst is as strong as your hunger, indulge in any of the great tequila-based cocktails, natural wines or bright, fresh juices.

Schaafstraat 4
Wednesday-Saturday 6pm-12am & Sunday 1am-11pm
+31 64 084 8875

drinks. dinner.

cornerstore

Amsterdam Noord is the place to be for all things hip & happening. This formerly overlooked corner of the city has had a serious renaissance in the last few years, and it's only getting better. One of the newest additions to our new favourite 'hood is cornerstore. This charming restaurant has a menu heaving with fantastic natural wines & Asian-inspired bites.

Papaverweg 11
Wednesday-Thursday 6.30pm-1am & Friday-Saturday 6pm-1am
+31 20 239 0062

drinks. lunch. dinner. takeout.

Euro Pizza Restaurant & Restaurant Europa

Killer croquettes? No problem! Great coffee? Easy! But pizza? Well, that's a different story here in Amsterdam. Or at least it used to be until Euro Pizza burst onto the scene in the midst of the hellfire of 2020. This laid-back restaurant is good for more than just excellent pizza, however. Head here for delicious natural wines & thoughtful small plates, or snag a table at their sister spot, Restaurant Europa, next door.

Gedempt Hamerkanaal 79-81
Europizza: Tuesday-Friday 6-11pm & Saturday 1-11pm
& Sunday 1-9pm
Restaurant Europa: Thursday-Saturday 6-11pm
& Sunday 1-7pm
+31 20 895 0843

dinner. shop.

Hotel de Goudfazant

What was once a bare-bones car garage has been miraculously transformed into an elegant, industrial, gourmet restaurant. Though we'd never say no to a cosy, intimate dinner at Hotel de Goudfazant, it's one of the best places in town to head with a big group. Wear your loosest trousers because you won't be able to resist ordering all of the delicious seafood on the menu.

Aambeeldstraat 30
Tuesday-Sunday 6pm-12am
+31 20 636 5170

get groovy

drinks. dinner. dancing.

Skatecafé

You are guaranteed to feel hip when you cross the threshold at this trendy bar & restaurant in Amsterdam Noord. It is a great place to have a chill, vibey dinner with a large group of friends, thanks in no small part to the indoor skate park. Watch the skaters ollie and heel flip for hours while you sip an ice-cold beer.

Gedempt Hamerkanaal 42
Thursday 3pm-1am & Friday-Saturday 3pm-3am
+31 20 210 0232

get shopping

lunch. drinks. shop.

Fromagerie Abraham Kef & Proeflokaal Kef

Is there a better combination than wine & cheese? If you ask us, there most definitely is not. When a hankering for a few pieces of creamy, funky cheese & an intriguing wine creeps up, hop on your bike and whizz over to Proeflokaal Kef or their shop, Fromagerie Abraham Kef, that's just next door. Their location in Noord has a large tasting room & gorgeous terrace – the ideal place to indulge in a cheese tasting.

Van der Pekplein 1b
Fromagerie: Tuesday-Saturday 10am-6pm & Sunday 12-6pm
Proeflokaal: Thursday 3-9pm & Friday-Saturday 12-9pm & Sunday 12-8pm
+31 20 737 0817

shop.

CHATEAU KARLITO

Just like Noord itself, Chateau Karlito is a wonderful whirling dervish, managing to pack a lot of things – wines, ceramics, rugs, jazz, sake, sausages, cider – into one cute, inviting shop. Sure, it may sound chaotic, but that's what we love about it. As Chateau Karlito's eponymous owner hails from Brabant (home of *Brabantsche worstenbroodje*), you know their sausage rolls just have to be good.

Van der Pekstraat 72
Wednesday-Saturday 11am-6.30pm

get cultured

lunch. shop. culture.

Eye Filmmuseum

Whether you're heading to the Eye Filmmuseum to catch a killer exhibition, a screening of an unusual movie or simply to snap a photo of its beautiful design, you will not be disappointed. We like to settle into their café with a coffee (or a drink!) to enjoy the sweeping views of the IJ. If you have a Cineville card or Museumkaart, you'll get a little discount on your tickets.

IJpromenade 11
Monday-Thursday 10-12am & Friday-Saturday 10-1am & Sunday 10-12am
+31 20 589 1400

drinks. dinner. culture.

FC Hyena

Going to the movie theatre is almost always a good idea. It's an even better idea when you can tuck into fresh, simple food & lovely, organic wines before you head into the relaxing cavern of the theatre. FC Hyena is a cool neighbourhood cinema showing art house films. Haven't managed to finish that bottle before the movie starts? No problem! You're free to bring it in with you.

Aambeeldstraat 24
Please check their website for current show times
+31 20 363 8502

culture.

Nxt Museum

Though we're real suckers for beautiful works by Old Masters like Vermeer and Paulus Potter, we've been on a bit of a new media art kick lately. When we want to scratch that tech-y itch, we like popping into Nxt Museum. It's got wonderful rotating exhibitions that focus on large-scale, multi-sensory works. Even if you're more old school, we bet you're going to love this.

Asterweg 22
Monday-Tuesday 11am-8.30pm & Wednesday 11am-9.30pm & Thursday-Saturday 11am-10.30pm & Sunday 11am-8.30pm

DE PLANTAGE & DE OOSTELIJKE EILANDEN

Walking or cycling along the canals – especially at sunrise or sunset – is truly magical.
If you've got the time, find a spot on one of Amsterdam's many bridges and watch the boats pass by.

GET TO KNOW DE PLANTAGE & DE OOSTELIJKE EILANDEN

To know De Plantage and Oostelijke Eilanden is to love them. Just a stone's throw from both Oost and Grachtengordel, these lush, leafy neighbourhoods really have the best of both worlds. Verdant and stately with a boon of charming corners and impressive buildings, De Plantage & Oostelijke Eilanden are cradled by the Amstel and the IJ. Though the energy of the canal belt can certainly be invigorating, we love escaping to De Plantage & Oostelijke Eilanden to meander through their shady boulevards, elegant squares and sweet, charming alleyways. Wherever we go in these enchanting neighbourhoods, we feel as if we've entered another world.

And while we can often be found simply breezing through the area with a coffee in hand, what we adore most about De Plantage & Oostelijke Eilanden is the culture. Here, it rules the roost. Whether we're taking note of unfamiliar species at the botanical gardens, taking in art historical gems at the H'ART Museum or just taking it easy in one of the area's lovely parks, we are never bored. It's no wonder this beautiful, peaceful 'hood is known as the cultural garden of Amsterdam. De Plantage & Oostelijke Eilanden are ideal for those looking to get cultured and get back to nature.

Yvo van Regteren Altena & Jort Kelder

gloobles curators De Plantage & Oostelijke Eilanden

While they may be self-dubbed snobs, Yvo van Regteren Altena and Jort Kelder are really anything but. Humble, sharp and wildly engaging, the pair know both a good time and great taste. When they're not crafting enigmatic perfumes, captivating articles or the ideal dinner party guest list, Yvo & Jort are determining what's chic and what isn't on The Snobcast. These two are the consummate authorities on all things elegant.

"Just 250 metres over the Amstel, and all of a sudden, the tourists are gone."

Even though we travel quite a lot ourselves, neither of us wanted to live somewhere overrun by tourists. It may not be very logical, but we don't want to see any tourists when we're at home. About 10 or 15 years ago, tourism really started to boom, particularly in the canal ring, so it felt like the right time to move out of the centre and into another area.

Some family members lived over in De Plantage, and we started to explore the area a bit more on Sunday strolls. Just 250 metres over the Amstel, and all of a sudden, the tourists are gone.

The nice thing is that when you are here, when you close your doors and open your windows, it's like you are living in the countryside. You have all this green and these beautiful inner gardens, but if you get on your bike, you're back in the bustle of the city in three minutes. You can really escape in De Plantage; you almost forget you live in the middle of a chaotic capital city. In the early mornings, you can hear the gibbons from Artis. You do your workout, and you have a private little communion with the elephants.

In the last decade, the neighbourhood has really evolved in a great way. There are many wonderful independent shops and restaurants that give the area so much character. There's a very nice greengrocer that has all the little delicacies we love. There are places where you can still buy CDs, which is very old-fashioned but great for grey old men like us. You have independent bookstores. I'm always scared these types of places will disappear, but they seem to really thrive here.

We have this podcast called The Snobcast, so as you can imagine we're both quite snobby. And while you'd think that a snob should live on the Prinsengracht or the Keizersgracht, it actually makes so much more sense for us to be in De Plantage, in a neighbourhood where you get a lot of space rather than three tiny rooms and lots and lots of stairs.

And that's the charming thing about this neighbourhood. When you want to be in it, in the thick of things in the city, you're just across the river. But you feel as if you're a world away.

Tessa Duste

gloobles curator De Plantage & Oostelijke Eilanden

An intrepid traveller from a young age, Tessa always found herself drawn to both the hustle and bustle of the city and the peace and quiet of nature. This dichotomy is evident in how she spends her time—helming Makers of Sustainable Spaces (MOSS), a company dedicated to restoring natural balance by adding greenery to city environments. Unsurprisingly, Tessa embodies this duality when she travels and when she's at home; she's got intel on the ideal kitesurfing spots but can also lead you to the coolest underground parties for a good boogie. Tessa knows how to live and travel outside of the box.

"I urge you to embrace the spirit of exploration and let these hidden gems surprise you."

With my recent move from De Pijp to Oost, I am excited to whisk you away on an enchanting adventure through the neighbourhoods of De Plantage and Oostelijke Eilanden, where a tapestry of history, culture and creativity awaits.

Let's begin our escapade in the elegant embrace of De Plantage. This leafy district is a tranquil oasis nestled within the bustling heart of Amsterdam. Strolling through the lush Hortus Botanicus, the city's botanical garden, you'll be enchanted by the vibrant blooms and rare plants that grace your path.

Next, wander towards the Royal Zoo, Artis, a true jewel of De Plantage. Here, you can embark on an animalistic odyssey, encountering a vast array of species from around the globe. Immerse yourself in the rich history of this remarkable institution, which dates back to 1838. Whilst you're there, don't forget to discover the laid-back gem Café-Restaurant De Plantage. Tucked away amidst the greenery of the Artis Royal Zoo, this restaurant is captivating. From their hearty breakfasts to their delectable dinners, the menu features both classic and innovative dishes.

As we venture eastward, Oostelijke Eilanden unveils an enchanting blend of old and new, where the past seamlessly intertwines with the future. This once-industrial neighbourhood has undergone a remarkable transformation, evolving into a vibrant hub of contemporary architecture, creative dining and cultural vitality.

For a taste of the artistic soul that permeates these neighbourhoods, make your way to the Lloyd Hotel & Cultural Embassy. This historic building has been meticulously restored and transformed into a great low-cost hotel and cultural hotspot. With its eclectic blend of artistic installations, exhibitions and events, the Lloyd Hotel serves as a lively nexus where creativity blossoms.

For those seeking an unforgettable Dutch experience in the area, 't IJ Brewery is a must-visit. Situated in a former bathhouse, this brewery combines history and flavour to create a unique culinary adventure. Try their exceptional range of craft beers. Last but certainly not least, let's end our culinary escapade at Scheepskameel. This contemporary eatery in the Eastern Docklands effortlessly marries Dutch and French cuisines.

As our adventure through De Plantage and Oostelijke Eilanden comes to a close, I urge you to embrace the spirit of exploration and let these hidden gems surprise you. Amsterdam never fails to amaze with its ability to blend old-world charm and contemporary flair. So, slip into your most stylish walking shoes, and prepare for a journey through the east side.

Zuzia Batolik

gloobles curator De Plantage & Oostelijke Eilanden

When people talk about 'doing it all', we can't help but think of our adorable friend Zuzia. Raised in Poland but based in Amsterdam, this full-time psychology student also happens to be a content creator, consummate cook and serial supper clubber hell-bent on creating connection through food. When she's on the road, Zuzia rarely has any real agenda. She loves to simply fold into local life, soaking up a city's vibe from a cute corner café. Come to Zuzia for wonderful wine bars, all things delicious and the perfect spots to snap a great photo.

"Every time I step outside to walk my dog, I fall in love with the peacefulness of my street."

About three years ago, I moved to Amsterdam, and I have lived in the eastern part of the city ever since. When I found my current apartment in De Plantage two years ago, the neighbourhood really captured my heart and soul. Every time I step outside to walk my dog, I fall in love with the peacefulness of my street. It's like being in my own little green paradise, surrounded by nature. On one side, I've got the chill vibes of the Wertheimpark, which is a small heaven for our furry friends; and on the other side, the beautiful energy of Artis.

Mornings are the most beautiful when I see the city waking up, accompanied by the song of the animals at Artis. The botanical garden gets busier and local cafés fill up with familiar faces. Since day one, I have always adored the fact that my neighbours greet each other. Even though I may not know the name of the woman I run into regularly, we never pass each other without exchanging a friendly greeting—which really underscores the strong sense of community in De Plantage. In the summertime, the area around the Entrepotdok is packed with people enjoying the sun and swimming in the canals. From June onwards, I spend most of my weekends by the water, reading a book or having a drink at Gollem Aan Het Water.

Speaking of drinks, there's also my favourite brown bar Café de Druif. This place is our local heaven. You can enjoy a classic late breakfast like a croissant or a *broodje kaas* (cheese sandwich) with mustard and pickles on the side. If you feel like grabbing a drink in the afternoon, you can head to de Druif and stay until late; they even have a selection of natural wines if you're up for sharing a bottle. Another spot for a seasonal bite and great wine is definitely Apollonia, vis-à-vis Nemo Science Museum. If drinks with friends transition into dinner, there's always Restaurant Entrepot—one of my favourites. The interior and the open kitchen make the atmosphere unique, and both the wine and food are excellent.

Another important and convenient feature of De Plantage is that we have a variety of laptop-friendly places to get some work done. For me, it's either Coffee Company on the sunny corner of Plantage Muidergracht or Café-Restaurant De Plantage. I love studying or answering emails there with a glass of wine in the evenings. It's a great motivation boost if I need a break from working at home. Exploring this neighbourhood is one of my favourite activities, as there is always something new popping up that I immediately add to my long list of places to check out. One of them, which isn't new but definitely worth a try, is Scheepskameel over in Oostelijke Eilanden.

There are just so many amazing spots around here. It's wonderful to chill at local spots that aren't invaded by tourists. And the cherry on top? They're just a 10-minute bike ride away from busy Centrum. So, whenever I feel like hanging out with friends outside of my area, I can get on my bike and be there in no time. It offers an ideal balance of local charm and city excitement.

oosterdokskade
prins hendrikkade
dijksgracht
piet heinkade
kattenburgerstraat
grote wittenburgerstraat
oostenburgermiddenstraat
conradstraat
wittenburgergracht
hoogte kadijk
entrepotdok
uilenburgerstraat
valkenburgerstraat
artis
plantage middenlaan
plantage muidergracht
sarphatistraat
mauritskade
nieuwe prinsengracht
weesperstraat
linnaeusstraat
oosterpark
ruyschstraat
eerste oosterparkstraat
beukenweg
populierensweg
amsteldijk
amstel
weesperzijde

DE PLANTAGE & DE OOSTELIJKE EILANDEN

get breakfast

breakfast. coffee. lunch.

Dignita Hoftuin

This stunning all-glass café is nestled snugly in the back garden of Amsterdam's H'ART Museum. After an hour or two in the museum, we love settling in for a relaxed lunch or a coffee. They've got wonderful fresh, healthy salads & sandwiches, all featuring vegetables from their gardens. It's also one of our top spots for a luxurious weekend brunch.

Nieuwe Herengracht 18a
Monday-Sunday 9am-5pm
+31 20 370 2723

get lunch

lunch. drinks. dinner.

Apollonia

Truly unpretentious, Apollonia is one of the dreamiest spots for a late spring or summer lunch in the city. We like to settle in on their sun-drenched terrace perched on Marineterrein for creative sandwiches, natural wines and delicious small bites. While we like it best at lunchtime, it's also great for breakfast (from 10am), *aperitivi* or dinner.

Kattenburgerstraat 5, 27e
Wednesday-Thursday 6pm-12am & Friday-Saturday 12pm-12am
+31 68 159 9871

get dinner

dinner.

Coulisse

Casual but still cosy, Coulisse is the kind of place you can easily envision becoming part of your dining out routine; it's also great for special occasions. Like so many of our go-to spots, Coulisse is hyper-focused on sourcing quality ingredients from local farmers, fishermen & producers. That means, whatever you're eating—spring, summer or fall—it's going to be fresh, fresh, fresh.

Oostenburgergracht 75
Tuesday-Thursday 6.30pm-12am & Friday 7pm-12am
& Saturday 5pm-12.30am
+31 20 737 1007

drinks. dinner.

Foer

Culinary veterans Maitre Juriaan van der Maarel (from gloobles favourite Rijsel) & Steven Broere have crafted an absolute delight of a restaurant in Foer. The name hints at the Dutch verb *foerageren*, so it should come as no surprise that the menu leans heavily on seasonal produce from the Netherlands, with the menu changing from top to bottom every two months.

Cruquiusweg 9
Monday 6pm-12am & Wednesday 6pm-12am
& Thursday-Sunday 2pm-12am
+31 20 846 2881

drinks. dinner.

Restaurant Entrepot

Beautifully situated at the crux of two little canals, Restaurant Entrepot is stunning before you even step inside. The interior, like many of our favourite restaurants in the city, is sleek and pared back with an industrial edge. The food employs similar restraint, elevating simple, fresh local ingredients and pairing them with an exciting, dynamic wine list. You could come here weekly and never get bored.

Entrepotdok 7
Wednesday-Thursday 6-11pm & Friday-Saturday 6pm-1am
& Sunday 6-11pm
+31 20 341 5722

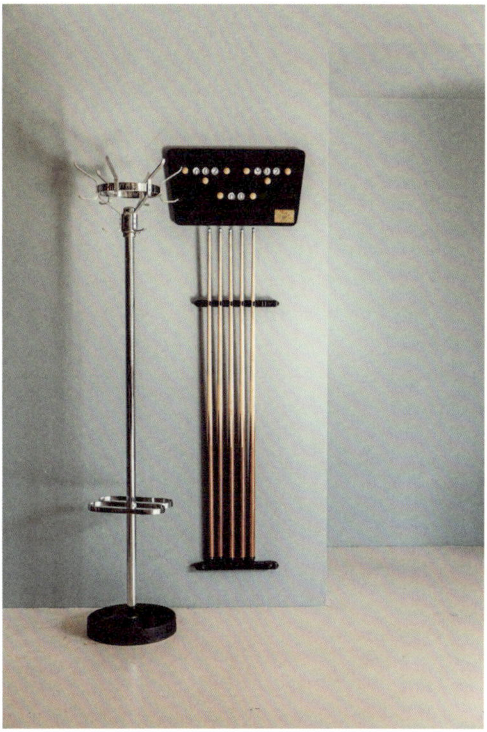

ENTREPOT

WC

drinks. dinner. takeout.

Scheepskameel

Good luck pronouncing the name of this trendy, spacious restaurant if you're not a native speaker. But luckily, your mouth will be far better occupied gobbling up the simple yet delicious food. Because it's an expansive yet inviting room, it's a great place to dine with a group–they'll also do a well-priced set menu for you. The fact that the killer wine list is jam-packed with excellent German wines only makes it all the more appealing.

Gebouw 024A Kattenburgerstraat 5
Tuesday-Thursday 6pm-12am & Friday-Saturday 6pm-1am
+31 20 337 9680

drinks. dinner. shop.

V R R & Stadsbakkerij As

Hotel de Goudfazant is a behemoth in the Amsterdam culinary scene. Anyone who's into food has dined there, and if they haven't, they're too shy to admit it. The power team behind this legend have joined forces with one of the city's best bakeries, Stadsbakkerij As, to open a terrific casual Dutch restaurant. It's open for dinner during the week, but we're particularly partial to a long, leisurely Sunday lunch.

Conradstraat 471
restaurant: Tuesday-Sunday 6pm-12am
bakery: Tuesday-Saturday 9am-3pm

V R R

get cultured

activity. culture.

ARTIS

“At Artis, be sure to swing by the building housing the small, friendly monkeys who’ll climb around (or on!) you.”

— Tessa

Let’s face it – not every zoo in every city is worth visiting. In fact, we’d wager that most of them don’t hold any particular appeal for anyone over the age of nine. ARTIS, however, is a totally different story. It is a true gem. One of the oldest zoos in Europe – and the oldest in the Netherlands – ARTIS is both beautiful & educational. Make sure to check out its botanical garden – and grab a drink at Serre while you peep the penguins – when you’re there.

Plantage Kerklaan 38-40
Monday-Sunday 9am-6pm (in summer)
Monday-Sunday 9am-5pm (in winter)

culture.

H'ART MUSEUM

Though a lot of Amsterdam's museums are clustered together in the Museumkwartier, one of our go-to spots for soaking up culture is just across the Magere Brug. Thanks to partnerships with the British museum, Centre Pompidou and Smithsonian American Art Museum, H'ART has a dizzying rotation of stellar exhibitions throughout the year. Visiting on a Saturday? Check out the lovely market on Saturdays to scoop up fresh groceries for the week.

Amstel 51
Monday-Sunday 10am-5pm
+31 20 530 8755

coffee. lunch. culture.

Hortus Botanicus

Since you're already in one of Amsterdam's greenest, leafiest neighbourhoods, why not go whole hog? Step out of the city and into the wild at the Hortus Botanicus. Whether it's a rare sunny day or bucketing down outside, you'll be transported to a tropical paradise. As it's right around the corner from ARTIS, we love to hit both in one day.

Plantage Middenlaan 2a
Monday-Sunday 10am-5pm
(in summer: Monday-Wednesday 10am-5pm
& Thursday-Sunday 10am-9pm)
+31 0 625 9021

OOST & WATER-GRAAFSMEER

If you are looking for a leafier, greener view,
hop on your bike and head across the Amstel to Oost & Watergraafsmeer.

GET TO KNOW OOST & WATER-GRAAFSMEER

If you've been to Brooklyn or Shoreditch, you'll have at least a semblance of an idea what Amsterdam's Oost & Watergraafsmeer are like. They're up-and-coming, they make room for new places & new ideas and they're a true melting pot. Though they may not be overflowing with quite as many hotspots as Noord or Grachtengordel, Oost & Watergraafsmeer are still chock-full of hidden gems, as well as some of the most wonderful parks & festivals in the city.

It can feel like a bit of a trek on foot, depending on what the weather's like and where you're coming from. That's why biking is our favourite way to head east to check out fun cafés like Rum Baba, peruse the Dappermarkt, play a round of tennis in the Oosterpark or experiment with some unusual, natural wines at Bottleshop. Wherever you go, Oost & Watergraafsmeer feel new & exciting—they were only officially established by the municipality back in 2010, in fact. So, slip into your sneakers and get ready to feel like the queen (or king!) of cool.

Eben Badu

gloobles curator Oost & Watergraafsmeer

A true creative. An innovator. Eben is so far outside of any box you could imagine. Well, except the box a pair of The New Originals x Dechase boots come in, of course. Just like his brand TNO, Eben is Amsterdam through and through. But also just like TNO, he's collaborative, dynamic and keen to expand horizons wherever he can. Though he's often travelling for work, work is truly pleasure for him. He loves really digging into a place, finding out how the locals do it and doing it right alongside them. Come to him for the very best tips for dining, dreaming, DJing and doing travel the right way.

"Different restaurants. Different music. It's a super unique area."

I was born and raised in Amsterdam Oost; I still live there today, in fact. So, I obviously really love the neighbourhood. It's a part of the city that perfectly represents the bubble I exist in, the world I've been a part of. Unlike many other parts of Amsterdam, Oost is very diverse. It feels like its own city within a city; when you're there, you kind of feel like you're not even in Amsterdam anymore. In a good way, of course.

You can find many different nationalities there, which means you can find all different types of people there. Different music. Different restaurants with different cuisines. I'm Ghanaian, so it's really cool to live somewhere you can find lots of great Ghanain restaurants. I never miss one when I travel, so it's great to be able to get those classic dishes in my own city too.

All of Oost and all its little pockets make it a super unique area.

Oost is also very close to Centrum, which is amazing. You can hop into town really easily (you can get to pretty much all other parts of the city super quickly). It feels removed but connected, which I like a lot.

Living in Oost is like living in your own little hideout away from all the chaos.

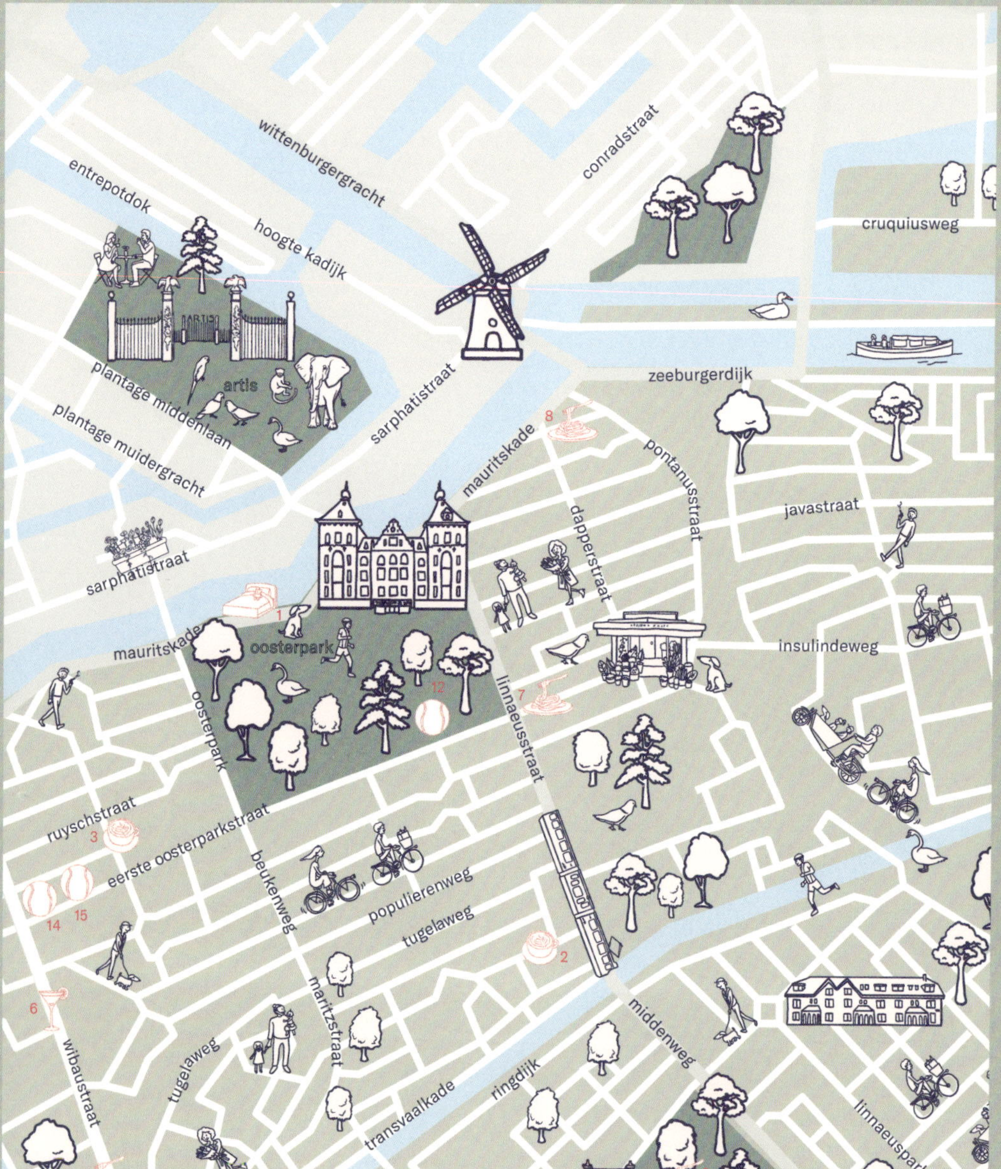
entrepotdok
wittenburgergracht
hoogte kadijk
conradstraat
cruquiusweg
artis
plantage middenlaan
plantage muidergracht
sarphatistraat
zeeburgerdijk
8
mauritskade
pontanusstraat
dapperstraat
javastraat
sarphatistraat
1
mauritskade
oosterpark
insulindeweg
12
7
linnaeusstraat
oosterpark
ruyschstraat
3
eerste oosterparkstraat
14
15
beukenweg
populierenweg
tugelaweg
2
6
middenweg
maritzstraat
tugelaweg
wibautstraat
transvaalkade
ringdijk
linnaeusparkweg
11
9
weesperzijde
4
5
wibautstraat
frankendael park
13
10
middenweg
amstel
gooiseweg

OOST & WATERGRAAFSMEER

get sleepy

sleep. breakfast. coffee. lunch. drinks. dinner.

Pillows Maurits at the Park

Over the last few years, we've spent more and more time in Oost thanks to stellar restaurants, charming bars and some of our favourite museums in the city. Now that Pillows Maurits at the Park has opened up, we think we just might be moving in. This grand hotel has sweeping ceilings and thoughtful details, but, thankfully, it remains intimate and relaxed. Vacation or staycation, you cannot go wrong with Pillows.

Mauritskade 61
+31 20 802 0200

get coffee

coffee. takeout. shop.

Rum Baba – Oost

This coffee roaster & bakery has a couple locations in town, but our fave spot is their location on the Pretoriusstraat. Of course, we can never resist a freshly roasted coffee, but their homemade cakes are just as dangerously delicious. Ditto for their sister café Coffee Bru, which is just around the corner. Hooked on their beans after a few visits? There's no need to make the trip when you run out. You can order their fresh-roasted coffee online or visit their café on Elandsgracht.

Pretoriusstraat 15
Monday-Thursday 7.30am-4.30pm; Friday 7.30am-5pm & Saturday 8am-5pm & & Sunday 8.30am-5pm

coffee. drinks. takeout.

4850

During the day, this cool little spot is the perfect place to pick up a coffee & an excellent cinnamon bun–here they call them *kanelbullar*–to take with you to the Oosterpark. No one here would judge you if you snagged an extra (or perhaps a bag full of 'em) to store in the freezer for "emergencies".

Camperstraat 48-50
Monday-Thursday 9am-3pm & Friday-Sunday 9am-6pm
+31 20 786 1041

get lunch

sleep. coffee. lunch. drinks. dinner.

De Vergulden Eenhoorn

When the sun is shining, Amsterdam's population seems to swell; suddenly, people are everywhere. On roofs. In parks. On terraces. That's why, occasionally, we prefer to escape the madness of the centre and head out to this gorgeous former farm. Sitting pretty on a sweet canal, De Vergulden Eenhoorn feels a world away from it all. Treat yourself to a night in one of their lovely rooms and wake up feeling refreshed & renewed.

Ringdijk 58
Monday-Sunday 10am-12am
+31 20 214 9333

breakfast. coffee. lunch. dinner.

Restaurant Merkelbach

If you've got a bike, then the 15-minute ride from city centre out to Park Frankendael is more than worth it. This restaurant is housed in a grand home and boasts a sunny terrace in a romantic garden. The chef is part of the Slow Food Movement, churning out dishes with authentic, sustainably produced, regional & seasonal ingredients. Be sure to come hungry.

Middenweg 72
Monday-Sunday 9am-6pm
+31 20 665 0880

get drinks

drinks. dinner.

Bottleshop

It's easy to fly right past Bottleshop on your bike and never notice it's there. But that, my friend, would be a serious shame. This refined, minimalist wine bar is sleek but still charming and has a fantastic menu of natural wines from around the world. Come by for a great bottle and some inventive small plates.

Wibautstraat 130
Tuesday 6-11pm & Wednesday-Thursday 6pm-12am & Friday 5pm-2am & Saturday 5pm-1am

get dinner

lunch. drinks. dinner.

Buurtcafé De Tros

There's something incredibly appealing about a true neighbourhood haunt, a place where the local-est of locals hang on weekday evenings or weekend afternoons. Buurtcafé de Tros is a particularly charming iteration of "the local". Come by if you're in the mood for fresh, interesting natural wines, creative small plates and, our go-to order, a very good smash burger.

Linnaeusstraat 63h
Monday-Wednesday 5pm-12am & Thursday 12pm-12am & Friday-Saturday 12pm-1am & Sunday 12pm-12am

drinks. dinner.

Café Wu

Chef Timo de Beurs has turned his attention to a new, exciting venture: Café Wu. Inspired by classic Chinese cuisine, de Beurs' bistro takes a new approach with European techniques and ingredients. And while most people probably come for the food, the team at Café Wu have given extra special attention to the music. A groovy collection of vinyls and tapes blast through the speakers, making this place an absolute blast.

Dapperstraat 1
Tuesday-Thursday 6pm-12am & Friday-Saturday 6pm-1am
+31 20 224 6196

lunch. dinner.

De Kas

Because Amsterdam is a very casual city (you're infinitely more likely to see women zooming by on their bicycles in sneakers than heels), the restaurants tend to lean relaxed rather than elevated. That being said, the fine dining spots we do have are actually pretty spectacular. De Kas is one of the best. Situated in the former Amsterdam City Greenery, it has a daily changing menu with vegetables grown in their very own garden & greenhouse.

Frankendael Park, Kamerlingh Onneslaan 3
Monday-Saturday 12-4pm, 6pm-12am
+31 20 462 4562

dinner.

Restaurant Troef

Raymond Plat (you may remember him from 212), Niels Leijssenaar, Roderick Kunst and Willem Alberts have teamed up to create what will surely become an Amsterdam institution on par with Rijsel, De Kas or Buffet van Odette. The menu is à la carte—a bit of a rarity with the city's best restaurants these days—and focuses on French-ish dishes with a meander into Mediterranean flavours every now and again.

Schollenbrugstraat 8
Monday-Saturday 5.30-11.30pm
+31 62 982 7120

dinner.

Rijsel

The Netherlands may not be known for its gastronomic history, but luckily our dear Flemish neighbours are a slightly different story. Rijsel Rotisserie is a bright & airy restaurant with a bit of an industrial vibe that serves some of the tastiest food in town. Though all of their food is delicious, we find it impossible to resist their famous roast chicken.

Marcusstraat 52
Monday-Friday 6-10pm
+31 20 463 2142

get active

activity.

Oosterpark

This (sometimes) sunny park in Amsterdam's hip Oost neighbourhood has recently been revamped, and we barely recognise it. In a good way, of course! Pack up a picnic with provisions from the Dappermarkt and spend the afternoon people-watching before heading off to explore the 'hood. If it's a particularly steamy day, take a dip in the paddling pool or lounge under one of the park's many leafy trees to catch the breeze.

Oosterpark
open all day, every day

shop. activity.

Park Frankendael & De Pure Markt

This gorgeous park in Oost meanders gently over 7 acres of beautiful land. Back in the 1700s, the park was actually part of a wealthy estate, with gardens designed by landscape architect J.T.P. Bijhouwer. Known as the art and culture garden, Park Frankendael is a real draw because of its cultural, historical, ecological & botanical elements, as well as De Pure Markt, a special market that takes place every last Sunday of the month.

Park Frankendael
open all day, every day. check the website for De Pure Markt's current opening times.

activity.

PLTS – Oost

While New York, Los Angeles & London are certainly at the forefront of the boutique fitness studio revolution, we hold firm that Amsterdam is catching up quickly. PLTS is a sleek & stylish Pilates studio located in Amsterdam's Oost. Don't be fooled by the chill, calming décor (though we do love feeling like we're at the spa). The workout is seriously intense. We promise.

Eerste Oosterparkstraat 68
opening hours vary, so check the website for this week's schedule

DE PIJP & RIVIEREN-BUURT

Take a book, good wine & some snacks and lie in the grassy fields of the Sarphatipark, the cosiest park in Amsterdam!

GET TO KNOW DE PIJP & RIVIEREN-BUURT

For all its history, Amsterdam is quite a young, vibrant city. Sure, there are innumerable beautiful old buildings & incredible museums at every turn, but one thing we really love is its energy. While you can certainly find that verve in any of the neighbourhoods, there is nowhere it's more palpable than De Pijp & Rivierenbuurt. With their ever-changing streets and ever-growing roster of hotspots, De Pijp & Rivierenbuurt are pretty much Amsterdam's Latin Quarter. Beatnik flair abounds at every turn. Ever since these neighbourhoods began to flourish back in the 1960s, they have always been hubs for creative spirits, bohemians, students & young people from all walks of life. No matter where you go in Rivierenbuurt or De Pijp, there's always something happening: a pop-up art gallery, a terrace overflowing with lively, beautiful people, an unusual shop selling curios.

So, if you're aching for something fun & exciting, for a place that will never be the same from one day to the next, head south of the canal belt and spend a day exploring Rivierenbuurt and De Pijp.

Steve Musgrave

gloobles curator De Pijp & Rivierenbuurt

Half Dutch, half English and wholly unique, Steve has lived a very global life. With stints in Boston, London, Munich and Amsterdam, this bon vivant and serious storyteller certainly knows how to live well—and how to entertain a crowd. Keep your eye on Steve to get the dish on the best hotspots from Tel Aviv to Thailand.

"De Pijp has it all, from wonderful boutique shops & hipster cafés to a bounty of restaurants."

De Pijp has always been a core part of the fabric of Amsterdam. Its history is indelibly marked by the tribes who've come and gone for centuries, and this diversity makes it the delightful melting pot it is today. De Pijp has it all, from wonderful boutique shops & hipster cafés to a bounty of restaurants.

Originally called 'De Pijp' because of its narrow, pipe-like streets, this former working-class neighbourhood is now filled with trees, totally rejuvenated. It's a haven for convivial people, students luxuriating on *terrasjes* and people simply enjoying a few *biertjes* & some *bitterballen*.

The Albert Cuypmarkt is a must for a lazy stroll. Here, you can delve into a Dutch culinary experience: *lekkernijen* with *Hollandse nieuwe* (herring), as the inviting scent of freshly made *stroopwafels* waft your way. The gregarious stallholders give you an insight into *Amsterdamse* humour and always ensure a good laugh.

A favourite of mine is Scandinavian Embassy; they serve insanely good coffee and pastries. Perfect for a meander through the Sarphatipark's meticulously landscaped gardens. For lunch or dinner, I like Wijmpje Buikers. Beloved by locals, they serve honest, delicious food; the staff have even been dubbed 'the friendliest in Amsterdam'. I second that. Another outstanding spot is EN Japanese Kitchen & Sake Bar. This is THE PLACE. Ask for a table at the counter & watch the chefs work their magic. If continue further south, you may feel as if you're leaving postcard-worthy Amsterdam … think again, young Dora! Welcome to Rivierenbuurt.

Here, architecture changes quite drastically into the Amsterdam School and modernist New Pragmatism. It's far more residential than many other boroughs in Amsterdam, but it serves its locals well. The Maasstraat is the artery of Riverenbuurt; here you'll find the fantastic Sophie Eats and the best fruit & veg shop in Amsterdam, Fork. Do NOT enter if you're hungry.

When it comes to dinner, I adore Il Cavallino. They have great, affordable Italian food, and the staff always greet you with a heartfelt smile. If you score a table outside, you're in luck. It's a *gezellige* spot for a casual dinner. For a little more spice, Rasoi serves top-notch Indian food with a twist. I love this place!

I like strolling along the Amstel; if you walk far enough, you'll end up in Ouderkerk aan de Amstel. It's one of Amsterdam's best-kept secrets, as you can go for a swim & avoid the crowds. Amstel Boathouse is my favourite spot, as it has sun all day and serves great drinks and bites. You can even arrive by boat!

De Pijp & Rivierenbuurt are wonderful areas to explore and feel like a part of true Dutch life.

keizersgracht
kerkstraat
prinsengracht
reguliersgracht
prinsengracht
amstel
weesperstraat
nieuwe keizersgra
sarphatistraat
frederikspl.
lijnbaansgracht
weteringschans
mauritskade
nicolaas witsenkade
stadhouderskade
amsteldijk
weesperszijde
wibautstraat
ferdinand bolstraat
albert cuypstraat
van woustraat
amstel
ryusdaelkade
hans halsstraat
sarphatipark
ceintuurbaan
rustenburgerstraat
rustenburgerstraat
lutmastraat
talmastraat
jozef israëlskade
amstelkade
amstelkade
churchill-laan
scheldestraat
rijnstraat
kromme mijdrechtstraat
rooseveltlaan
uiterwaardenstraat
1
2
3
4
5
6
7
8
9
10
11
12
13
14
15
16
17

DE PIJP & RIVIERENBUURT

get drinks

drinks. shop.

Glouglou

If you spend even a few minutes wandering around De Pijp, you will definitely find somewhere to have a *biertje* or a glass of wine. But just because you could tumble into *a* bar at every step doesn't mean you shouldn't trot those extra centimetres to find *the* bar. Instead, we highly recommend heading to Glouglou, a fantastic wine bar just around the corner from the Sarphatipark. It's wonderfully inviting and serves top-notch natural, organic wines that are all free of additives.

Tweede van der Helststraat 3
Monday-Friday 3pm-12am & Saturday-Sunday 2pm-12am
+31 20 233 8642

LA PETITE BAIGNEUSE
JUSTE CIEL !
DE CUVE
2017
CLASSE
"A touch of class in a glass"
LE VIN DES
AMIS
Avanti popolo
Le temps des cerises
12% by vol
750 ml

get dinner

dinner.

Auberge

If you ever tire of Dutch food (mais, non!), fine-tuned, seriously delicious French cuisine is in order. But where to get such food? Auberge. The newest restaurant in Richard van Oostenbrugge and Thomas Groot's portfolio, Auberge takes what's already good–French food–and makes it even better. Ford the streams of tourists on the Albert Cuyp in search of some of the best French food in town. It's worth it!

Albert Cuypstraat 58-60
Monday-Sunday 12-2.30pm, 5.30-10pm
+31 20 845 2005

drinks. dinner.

Café Caron

This popular bistro is always buzzing, every single night of the week. The team at Café Caron has dreamed up a simple, straightforward menu of hearty French classics that makes even the coldest, drizzliest of evenings in Amsterdam cosy. Unlike many restaurants in the city, Café Caron is open late seven nights a week, so it's perfect when hunger strikes well after the sun has gone down.

Frans Halsstraat 28
Monday-Thursday 6pm-12am & Friday-Saturday 6pm-1am
& Sunday 12-3pm, 6pm-12am
+31 20 675 8668

drinks. dinner.

KID

Despite all the hype, KID somehow manages to maintain an air of mystery in Amsterdam's hospitality scene. An incredibly minimal Instagram. A vague website. Shrouded in secrets it may seem, but we're here to confirm: it's so, so delicious. With a stellar Asian-European menu built around the Indonesian and Chinese family dishes the owners grew up with, KID has cemented itself in Amsterdam's dining scene for good. And we couldn't be more thrilled.

Ruysdaelkade 251
Wednesday-Thursday 5.30pm-12.30am
& Friday-Saturday 5.30pm-1am & Sunday 5.30pm-12.30am

dinner.

Yamazato & Sazanka

As you step across the threshold at Yamazato or Sazanka, you'll likely be rubbing your eyes in disbelief. Were you just transported to Japan in the blink of an eye? Well, sort of. These Michelin-starred sister restaurants focus on the intricacies of omakase & teppanyaki dining, respectively. Whichever one you choose; you are in for a beautiful meal prepared with great attention to detail.

Hotel Okura, Ferdinand Bolstraat 333
Yamazato: Wednesday-Sunday 6-8pm
Sazanka: Monday-Tuesday 6-9pm & Thursday-Sunday 6-9pm
+31 20 6788 300

get shopping

shop.

Amélie Guépin

To be elegant but still stand out is a tough task, but Amélie Guépin makes it infinitely easier. A skilled couturier and seamstress, Amélie dreams up beautiful, timeless designs from her atelier in Oud-Zuid. Though we aren't lucky enough to have a wardrobe comprised entirely of her designs, it's our favourite spot for special pieces for special occasions.

Roerstraat 27
by appointment only
+31 62 951 3847

breakfast. coffee. shop.

Bakkerij Mater

What matters to us most on an early morning is a warm croissant and fresh slice of bread from Bakkerij Mater. Tucked away on the bustling Ceintuurbaan, Bakkerij Mater is a welcome haven in the middle of a busy street. After testing every new bakery in Amsterdam, we're inclined to say that Mater is the end all be all. High praise, yes, but well-deserved.

Ceintuurbaan 320 hs
Wednesday-Saturday 9am-4pm & Sunday 10am-4pm

shop.

De Aanzet

Ever since De Aanzet opened back in 1981, it's been THE place to scoop up beautiful organic produce and high quality products. The sweet neighbourhood grocer stocks brands like Yogi Tea, Landkrone, Luna e Terra and Whole Earth, in addition to the best local fruit and veg. Who needs the Albert Heijn when you have De Aanzet?!

Eerste Jacob van Campenstraat 10
Monday-Friday 8.30am-7pm & Saturday 8.30am-6pm
& Sunday 10am-5pm
+31 20 673 3415

takeout. shop.

Massimo Gelato – De Pijp

Amsterdam isn't warm & sunny year-round, but that doesn't mean *Amsterdammers* don't crave ice cream. Whenever we need a cool, sweet treat, we hop on our bikes and dash over to Massimo Gelato. With flavours like fresh summer peach & tangy, creamy ricotta, their gelato is truly the best. Save yourself a trip to Italy and grab a scoop here.

Van Ostadestraat 147h
Monday-Sunday 10am-11pm

shop.

Mevrouw Hamersma Kookboekwinkel

Wherever we are, wherever we go, we rarely miss an opportunity to check out charming local bookshops. There are many great ones in Amsterdam (Athenaeum, Van Rossum, Scheltema), but the most unique probably has to be Mevrouw Hamersma Kookboekenwinkel. Dedicated entirely to cookbooks, this charming shop is *the* spot for budding cooks and master chefs alike.

Gerard Doustraat 226
Friday-Saturday 11am-6pm
+31 20 771 6092

shop.

MOISE

We're of the mind that shopping is at its most delightful when you can source unique, high-quality pieces with ease. With fast fashion on the rise, that's not always so easy, but luckily MOISE is here to save the day. This luxury women's clothing store located on the Ceintuurbaan has an incredible, carefully curated selection of high-end women's clothes.

Ceintuurbaan 111
Tuesday-Saturday 10.30am-6pm
+31 61 123 5548

shop.

Veloretti

Amsterdammers are nothing without their bicycles. Join the pack (and outstrip 'em all in both style and speed) with a sleek, chic Veloretti. Go classic with one of their Robyns or Caféracers or enter the modern era with a super-cool, super-efficient electric bicycle. Or book the gloobles suite at De L'Europe and zip through town on a custom Veloretti.

Van Woustraat 72
Monday-Friday 9:30am-6pm & Saturday 10am-5:30pm
& Sunday 12-5pm
+31 20 261 1433

get beautiful

beauty.

Artist Lab

When you get a manicure done at Artist Lab, there's absolutely no need to come back a week later (we swear they really never chip). But the team is so lovely and the lacquer jobs so good that you just might be compelled. Want 10% off? Register to be a Venturer on gloobles.com.

Sarphatipark 22hs
Monday-Sunday 9am-9pm

get creative

coffee. creativity.

Clay Coffee

If we could quit our day jobs, we'd likely be beating down the doors at Clay Coffee asking them to hire us. This charming, sunny pottery studio hosts 5-week-long courses, as well as one-off sessions for events or team building. If you're not into making your own vessels, you can also sip a well-whisked matcha out of a beautiful, professionally made mug in their café.

Hemonylaan 6a
Monday-Friday 8.30am-4pm & Saturday 9am-5pm

OUD-ZUID

Some may say Oud-Zuid is a little sleepy,
but there's so much happening just below the surface.

GET TO KNOW OUD-ZUID

While we could agree that Amsterdam may be the more laid-back, casual sister when compared to Paris or London, that doesn't mean we can't do elegant. If you head to Oud-Zuid, you'll see exactly what we're talking about. This chic neighbourhood is pristine & well-manicured, boasting some of the most sophisticated buildings in the city.

Brimming with picturesque houses, wonderful boutiques like Azzurro Due & Skins Cosmetics and, of course, some of the best museums in the country, it's no wonder that this well-heeled 'hood is one of the most desirable areas to live in. But just because it's posh doesn't mean it's not as friendly as De Jordaan or De Pijp. Everyone in Oud-Zuid is warm & welcoming, ready to show you the gems hidden in their wonderful streets.

Judith Goudsmit

gloobles curator Oud-Zuid

After high school, Judith packed her bags and left Amsterdam for busy, bustling New York City to pursue her dream of writing and eating very, very well. Fast forward fifteen years, and Judith found herself back in Amsterdam, studying playwriting and trying her hand at just about every kind of odd job you could imagine. These days, you can find her writing plays, screenplays & teleplays in Amsterdam, New York or wherever a project may take her. Judith knows the best spots for a quick bite before a show or movie.

"If you want to escape the noise & madness of the centre, it can be a wonderful oasis."

My parents had always lived in the Nieuwmarkt neighbourhood, where my twin & I were born. But as the neighbourhood became more & more notorious for its red lights & sex shops, our parents decided it wasn't exactly child-friendly and moved to Oud-Zuid. We had a blissful childhood in those tree-lined streets – playing outside, roller-skating and a little bit of *belletje trekken* here & there.

After high school, I lived in New York, which is, in many ways, the opposite of the area where I grew up. The buzzing energy, the diversity in the streets, the sirens, the crowds – none of that can be found in Oud-Zuid. But being away for so long made me appreciate certain things about Oud-Zuid.

Even though a lot has changed over the years – the local vegetable and hardware stores made way for expensive clothing stores and posh lunchrooms – the trees, the Vondelpark, the calm remain the same. My parents have a subscription to the Sunday matinee concerts at the Concertgebouw, and when they aren't able to go, they often give me their tickets. Lucky me! There's nothing better than some wonderful classical music played by world renowned musicians to brighten a weekend. Afterwards, I always love to get a drink at the best neighbourhood bar, Café Welling. Apart from the Concertgebouw crowd, you will always find the regulars & bartenders who have been there for years and make the place feel homey & familiar.

When I have visitors come in from New York, we'll walk over to the Rijksmuseum or the Stedelijk Museum and roam around for a few hours. If we are in need of a coffee, we'll stop by Coffee District, which is actually owned by my cousin Rosa and her partner Adil. They already own two coffee shops in Oud-Zuid and are opening their third location near the Olympic Stadium, right next to the famous cheese shop l'Amuse and the French bakery Le Fournil de Sébastien.

I like to leave the neighbourhood for dinner; oftentimes, I go back to the Nieuwmarkt where my favourite Thai place O-cha is located or try out something new in Noord. But if I want to stay local, I love an Indian spot called Anjappar. Very spicy and delicious! When I want a nightcap, I like to go to Gruter, a typical brown café around the corner from my home. My grandmother always complained that the neighbourhood was changing – too many yuppies were ruining the neighbourhood – but like Welling, Gruter survived all those changes. She spent one of her last birthdays there with all her friends and got nice & tipsy! If I need something fried to soak up the alcohol, I'll go to snackbar Constantijn, to get myself a piping hot *kaassoufflé* before calling it a night.

Amsterdam Zuid might not be the reason you visit Amsterdam, but if you want to escape the noise & madness of the centre, it can be a wonderful oasis.

Hendrikje Crebolder & Taco Dibbits

gloobles curators Oud-Zuid

The world is a big place, and both Hendrikje and Taco have seen quite a lot of it. These days, however, they're both living in Amsterdam. While they're no longer colleagues (Taco is the General Director, whilst Hendrikje was the Director of Media & Development), they still share a great passion for Amsterdam's beautiful Museumkwartier. When they're not advising international art fairs or dreaming up creative programming, they're unravelling the secrets of their city. Naturally, they're founts of knowledge on all things art, but they've also got the lowdown on the best green spaces, coffee spots and shops, at home and abroad.

"There are big gardens behind the houses that you don't see as often in the canal belt."

When the Rijksmuseum was built, Oud-Zuid didn't exist. There are these very early photographs of the museum where you see green fields stretching beyond the building instead of the neighbourhood we know today. You would go from the city centre to what felt like the countryside simply by cycling beneath the museum. Today, there is still this incredible feeling of space there.

In Oud-Zuid, there is a lot of green and a lot of public space. There are big gardens behind the houses that you don't see as often in the canal belt. There are little sort-of-parks at the street crossings and, of course, the Vondelpark. It still really feels like a huge private garden despite being a true public space. You feel like you're in the countryside or in Hyde Park. They even have a wonderful concert series during the summer. Naturally, there's also the garden at the Rijksmuseum, which houses a great sculpture exhibition every year.

There's a lot of art and culture in the neighbourhood, which we really love. We have great colleagues around Museumplein like the Stedelijk Museum and the Van Gogh, as well as a lot of contemporary galleries and institutions that celebrate other disciplines like theatre and classical music. It's great to be a part of a cultured, international, fantastic environment. Oud-Zuid is sort of the cultural hub of the city.

A lot of the spots we like in the area have been around for a long time; they're real institutions. The brown cafés, for example. They're the kinds of places where you can really step into tradition and be a part of something, whether you're a local or a tourist. They're very close knit, but they're still very open. There are also some very nice places to eat in the neighbourhood. Of course, there's RIJKS and its sister restaurant WILS, but we also like this place Cucina Casalinga. It's this nice Italian restaurant we go to late in the evening sometimes. You walk in, and there are only Italians at the bar smoking big cigars.

All in all, it's just a lovely area. Beautiful architecture, very verdant and a little buzzy.

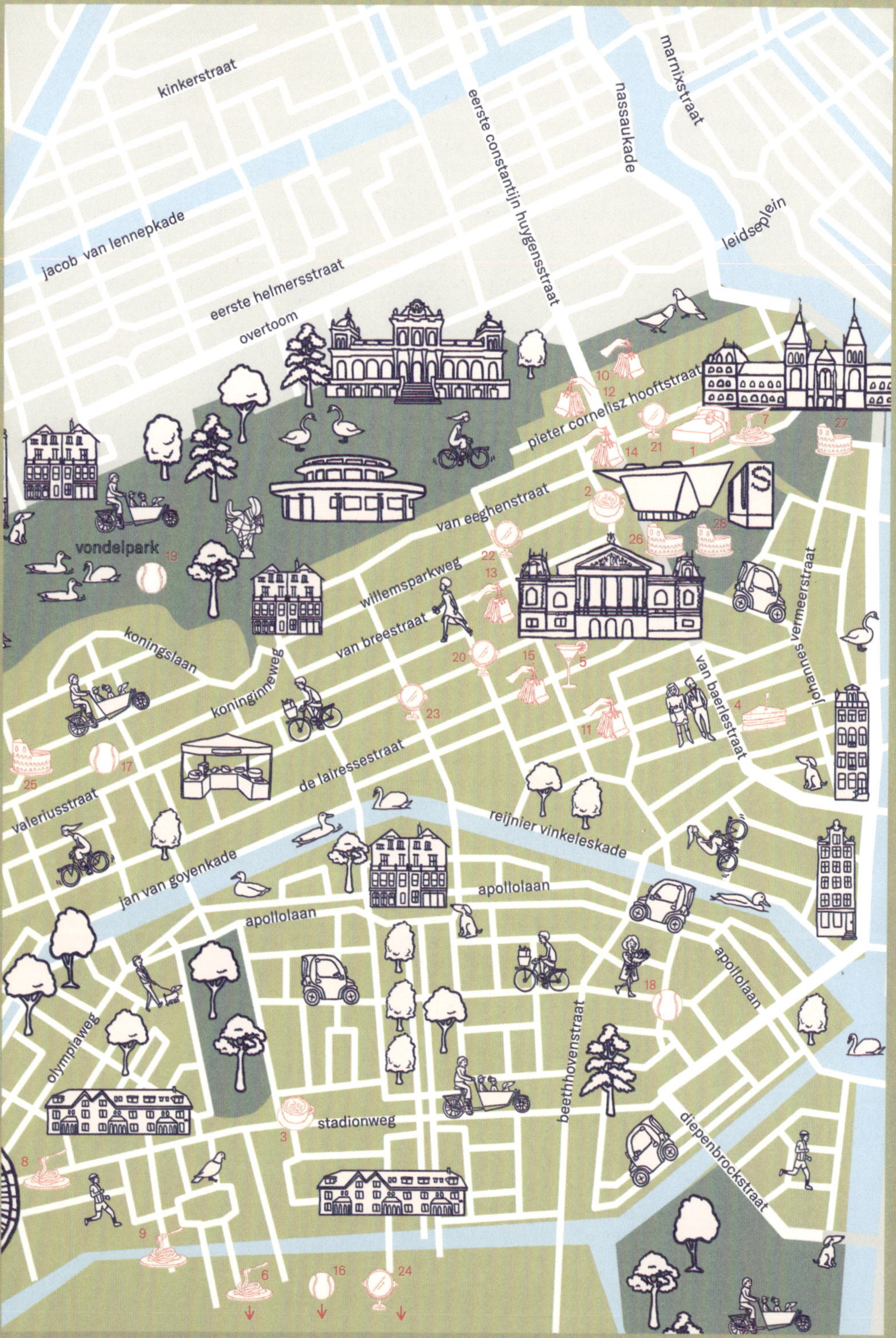
kinkerstraat
eerste constantijn huygensstraat
nassaukade
marnixstraat
leidseplein
jacob van lennepkade
eerste helmersstraat
overtoom
pieter cornelisz hooftstraat
van eeghenstraat
vondelpark
willemsparkweg
van breestraat
koningslaan
koninginneweg
johannes vermeerstraat
van baerlestraat
de lairessestraat
valeriusstraat
reijnier vinkeleskade
jan van goyenkade
apollolaan
apollolaan
apollolaan
olympiaweg
beethovenstraat
stadionweg
diepenbrockstraat
1
2
3
4
5
6
7
8
9
10
11
12
13
14
15
16
17
18
19
20
21
22
23
24
25
26
27
28

OUD-ZUID

get sleepy

sleep. coffee. drinks. shop. activity. beauty.

Conservatorium Hotel & Akasha

There are plenty of cute boutique hotels in Amsterdam, but if you're looking for a top-of-the-line hotel, you can't go wrong with the sumptuous Conservatorium. Located right next to the Museumplein & Amsterdam's own Rodeo Drive, the P.C. Hooftstraat, the Conservatorium is an ideal home base from which to explore the city. Treat yourself to a relaxing massage at their gorgeous spa, Akasha, or get your heart pumping in the sleek indoor swimming pool or state-of-the-art gym.

Paulus Potterstraat 50
+31 20 570 0000

get coffee

coffee. takeout.

Coffee District – Willemsparkweg

One of our perennial favourites for our morning jolt, Coffee District is beautiful & inviting whether you're lucky enough to snap up a spot on the bench outside or simply grabbing a cappuccino to-go. Not only is their coffee some of the best in town – and certainly some of the very best in the 'hood – but their pastries are also too moreish to resist. Snag a few extra chocolate chip cookies to bring home with you for when the craving inevitably strikes.

Willemsparkweg 8h
Monday-Friday 7.30am-4pm & Saturday-Sunday 8am-5pm
+31 64 820 0518

get lunch

“I love their Moroccan lentil soup, but their menu changes seasonally.”

— Judith

lunch. dinner. takeout.

Soup en Zo – Van Baerlestraat

We’re not really sure why, but we’ve always found it nearly impossible to find tasty, healthy food on-the-go. If more traditional fast food options aren’t tickling your fancy, you’re in luck, as Soup en Zo is just around the corner. They have a rotating selection of delicious, seasonal soups, as well as prepared salads. We love to grab a few containers whenever we go.

Van Baerlestraat 81
Monday-Friday 11am-8pm & Saturday 11am-7pm
& Sunday 12-7pm
+31 20 354 7497

get drinks

drinks.

Café Welling

While at first glance this may seem like any old brown café, we can assure you that Café Welling is actually so much more. Despite its humble appearance, Café Welling is a true scholarly round table, as many creatives & intellectuals have met here ever since it opened. It's also a wonderful spot to sip a beer after a classical concert at the Concertgebouw.

Jan Willem Brouwersstraat 32
Monday-Friday 4pm-1am & Saturday-Sunday 3pm-1am
+31 20 662 0155

get dinner

lunch. dinner.

Aan de Poel

While it's technically venturing out of the city (or at the very least on the way to an adventure), Aan de Poel is so good that even the slightly-longer-than-usual cycle feels manageable. Beautifully set on the water, this is the perfect spot for a special occasion. Elevated cuisine and a sweeping terrace are the makings of the ideal birthday, anniversary, graduation or just-a-Tuesday meal.

Handweg 1, Amstelveen
Tuesday-Thursday 12-4.30pm & 6-11pm, Friday 12-4.30pm & 6.30-11pm, Saturday 6-11pm
+31 20 345 1763

lunch. dinner.

RIJKS & WILS

When you hear the word RIJKS, your mind likely automatically heads to stunning still lifes & Dutch genre paintings. These days, though, there's even more to it. RIJKS is a great fine dining restaurant at the base of the museum with bright young chef Joris Bijdendijk at the helm. The restaurant focuses on seasonal ingredients and makes heavy use of vegetables from their garden. Craving something a bit more visceral? Head to their other spot, WILS, which harnesses the power of fire to craft their incredible dishes.

Museumstraat 2, Stadionplein 26
RIJKS: Tuesday-Sunday 11.30-2pm, 6-8.30pm
+31 20 674 7555
WILS: Tuesday 6-9.30pm
& Wednesday-Saturday 12-2.30pm, 6-9.30pm
+31 20 236 6522

dinner.

Umeno

We are so, SO grateful that there's been a boom in the number of great Japanese restaurants in Amsterdam in the past few years. There's a wonderful mix of casual and fancy, sushi and yakitori. When it's sushi we're after (and when we're fortunate enough to score a much-coveted reservation), Umeno has to be one of our top picks.

Agamemnonstraat 27
Wednesday-Saturday 7-11pm
+31 68 110 7899

get shopping

shop.

Azzurro Due

“Azzuro's staff is more than happy to spend hours with you finding the perfect outfit.”

— Zuzia

Though we hate to admit it, there aren't millions of good places to shop for stylish, unique clothing in Amsterdam. Luckily, this stylish city has one place that fits the bill, Azzurro Due. It's certainly the best place to stock your wardrobe with chic, interesting designer threads. Even the most ardent window shoppers are unlikely to come out empty-handed.

Van Baerlestraat 3
Tuesday-Saturday 10am-6pm & Sunday 12-6pm
+31 20 671 9708

coffee. lunch. takeout. shop.

Edible Treasures

Though it hasn't always been a haven for foodies, it's pretty safe to say Amsterdam is now a city for the seriously food obsessed. When gastronomes tire of eating at the city's finest, they turn to their own kitchens. And when they're ready to outfit those kitchens, they head straight for Edible Treasures. This lovely shop & deli has a top-notch selection of curated pieces for the kitchen, pantry & dining table.

Jacob Obrechtstraat 75
Tuesday-Saturday 10am-6pm

shop.

FOUR

There are a lot of very chic men in Amsterdam (really, who said Paris was the fashion capital of the world?), and if you follow any of them around for a while, they are sure to lead you to FOUR. This high-end menswear shop sells the newest & coolest designer clothing, as well as the trendiest shoes & accessories.

Van Baerlestraat 9-11
Monday 11am-6pm & Tuesday-Wednesday 10am-6pm & Thursday 10am-8pm Friday-Saturday 10am-6pm & Sunday 12-6pm
+31 20 6792244

shop.

Salon Heleen Hülsmann

At gloobles, we love a story. Especially when it comes to our clothing. That is why we find ourselves drifting into Salon Heleen Hülsmann again and again. With an unbelievable selection of pre-loved (used? Pffft!) clothing from brands like Alexander Wang and Alaïa, Heleen and her team never fail to deliver.

Jacob Obrechtstraat 18
by appointment only
+31 20 238 6965

shop.

Skins Cosmetics – Oud-Zuid

These days, our beauty regimes are just as essential as what we eat and how we exercise, if not more so. When you really want to treat yourself, pop into Skins Cosmetics to peruse the wide selection of unique perfumes & skincare products. Stuck on what kind of makeup will look best on you? Flag down a member of staff, as they are great at helping you choose the right products & shades.

Van Baerlestraat 27
Monday 12-7pm & Tuesday-Friday 10am-7pm
& Saturday 10am-6pm & Sunday 12-6pm
+31 20 528 6176

"There's always a line at Erik's, but all the guys who work there are hilarious & happy to help with all your cheesy needs."

— Hendrikje & Taco

takeout. shop.

ZuiderMRKT

Run by its host neighbourhood, Oud-Zuid, the ZuiderMRKT is a charming, bustling market bursting with fresh & organic products grown and crafted by local farmers. Every time we host a dinner party, we head straight to the ZuiderMRKT to buy our meat, veggies & dairy because we know it will always be of the highest quality.

Jacob Obrechtstraat & Johannes Verhulststraat
Saturday 9.30am-5pm

ALLINSON
2,85
SCONE
ROZIJNEN
2,10
WIT
2,85
POMPOEN/ROGGE
VOLKOREN
3,40
ROGGEKNAR
3,00
HEY
LEKKERE
MOP

get active

"Travelling with kids & want to take a break from the city hustle? Visit de Geitenboerderij in Amsterdamse Bos."

— Stephanie

activity.

Amsterdamse Bos

Don't get us wrong. We adore being in the city. There is no shortage of fantastic coffee shops or cool restaurants, but sometimes, we really need a breath of fresh air. Luckily, the Amsterdamse Bos is only a short zip on your bicycle away. Pack a picnic basket with goodies from Fromagerie Abraham Kef & levain et le vin and spend the day lounging in the sun and diving into the crisp, cool water.

Amsterdamse Bos, Amstelveen
open all day, every day

activity.

Bodyvita South

The team at Bodyvita truly believes that movement is life, and they strive to help their clients move through life with grace and ease thanks to their well-honed Pilates program. Though we like their original spot on the Kerkstraat, we prefer heading to their newer location in Oud-Zuid for a feeling of space and light.

Koninginneweg 145h
Monday-Friday 7am-10pm & Saturday-Sunday 9am-6pm
+31 63 313 1285

activity. culture.

Vondelpark

Escape the ever buzzing, ever chaotic city for a relaxed stroll through the popular Vondelpark. As it's the largest park in the city, there's always a corner to take it easy with a picnic or space on the path for an early morning jog. If flowers are your thing, you are sure to be delighted by the park's rose garden, which is home to more than 70 types of roses. Don't miss Picasso's fish statue or the wonderful music & dance performances at the open-air theatre in the summer.

Vondelpark
open all day, every day

get beautiful

shop. beauty.

Babassu – Oud-Zuid

This is a luxury beauty store & top-quality spa, all rolled into one. Living in, or visiting, a city can wreak havoc on your skin, so it's essential to have a good facialist on speed dial for skin emergencies. When you want to look as fresh as a Dutch tulip, book a facial at Babassu. We particularly like those done with Natura Bissé products. Not in the 'hood? Check out their Centrum location.

Cornelis Schuytstraat 40
Monday 9.30am-6pm & Tuesday 9.30am-9pm & Wednesday 9.30am-6pm & Thursday 9.30am-9pm & Friday 9.30am-6pm & Saturday 9.30am-5pm
+31 20 471 5148

beauty.

Bert Visser

Want to have the kind of haircut people envy? Book an appointment at Bert Visser. Great both on cut and colour, this chic salon ditches the chaotic energy so often found at hairdressers. Go in for a trim and come out looking fabulous. A glass of bubbles in the Conservatorium's bar after is the perfect way to celebrate a perfect hairdo.

Conservatorium Hotel, van Baerlestraat 27
Tuesday-Wednesday 10am-7pm & Thursday-Friday 10am-8pm & Saturday 10am-6pm
+31 20 673 7494

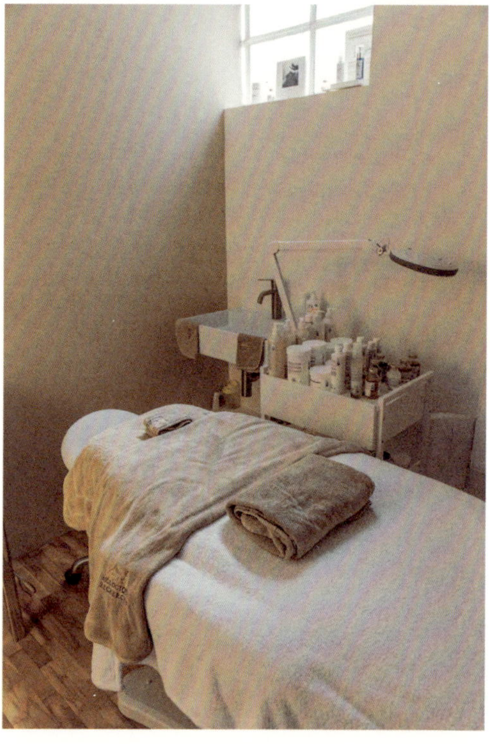

beauty.

Danny Diop – Jacob Obrechtstraat

There's no denying that having great skin is the quickest way to feel good pretty much all the time. Throw on sweats, slick your hair back and you still look amazing. The key to perfect skin in Amsterdam? Regular visits to Danny Diop. Book in for a Biologique Recherche facial or let Danny assess exactly what your skin needs. You're guaranteed to leave with a glow.

Jacob Obrechtstraat 14
Tuesday-Saturday 10am-6pm
+31 20 786 1051

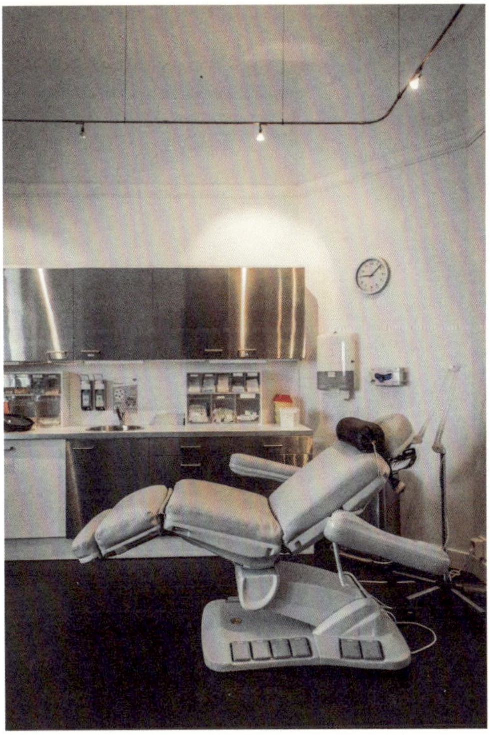

beauty.

Laser Centrum Cornelis Schuyt

A good facial is a transformative experience, but there's only so much a good cleanse and a great cream can do. For something a little deeper, a little more rejuvenating, book an appointment at Medical Laser Center on the Cornelis Schuytstraat. Though everyone on staff is talented and professional, we always book botox with Leonie and laser treatments with Tanja.

Cornelis Schuytstraat 55
Monday-Saturday 9am-5pm
+31 20 671 1379

activity. beauty.

Renessence

This stunning, serene space is like nowhere else we know in Amsterdam. Dedicated to true wellness, Renessence takes a holistic approach to health. Ice baths, floating, infrared sauna and cryotherapy are all on the menu for the bold. Want something a bit more relaxed? They also do fantastic massages and have a nice yoga programme.

George Gershwinlaan 520
Monday-Thursday 7am-9pm & Friday 7am-7pm
& Saturday-Sunday 9am-7pm
+31 20 303 8395

get cultured

culture.

EENWERK

The museums of Oud-Zuid aren't the only ones who rule the roost, despite how it may seem. This culture-soaked neighbourhood is also home to many a fantastic gallery. Chief amongst them is EENWERK. Designed by Barend Koolhaas & opened in 2017, this contemporary exhibition space has quickly become one of our favourite spots in the city.

Koninginneweg 176
Thursday-Saturday 1-6pm
+31 62 299 8772

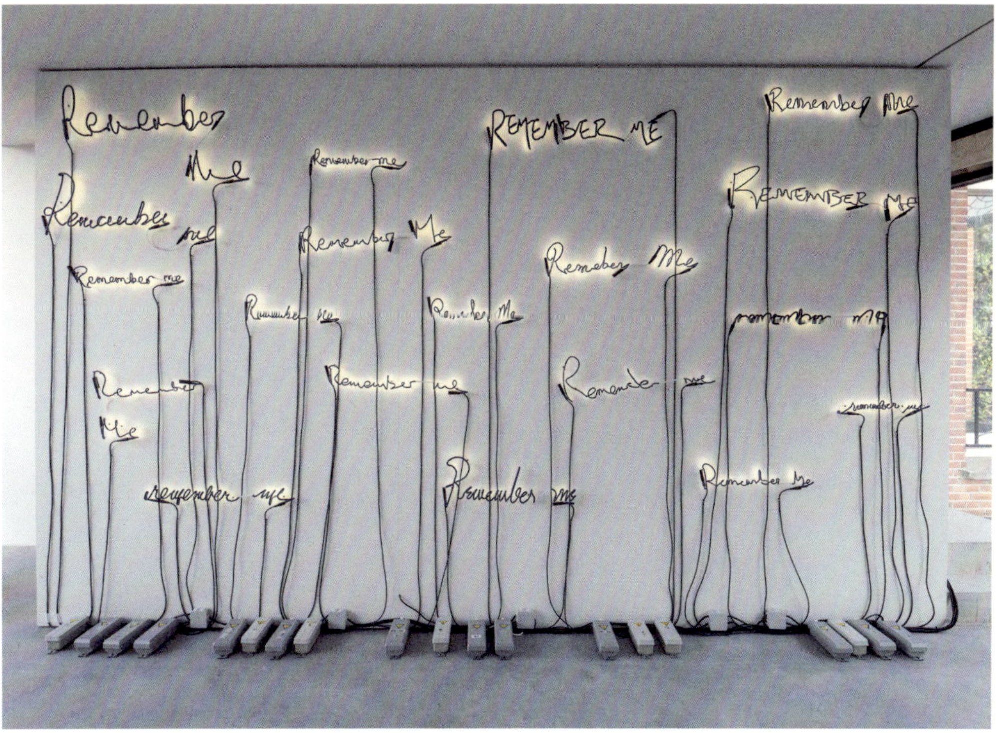

culture.

Het Concertgebouw

If you're not from Amsterdam, it's possible you might not have heard about the Concertgebouw, but it is truly one of the finest concert halls. Their resident orchestra, the KCO, is world renowned and always a treat to hear. We recommend perusing their website to see which concerts are coming up because they've got a diverse & ever-changing program.

Concertgebouwplein 10
opening hours vary, so check the website for concert times
+31 20 671 8345

"Be sure to check out the 17th-century dollhouses! They were my favourite when I was a little girl, but they never get old."

— Judith

coffee. shop. activity. culture.

Rijksmuseum

Whether you're in it for the artwork, the building or the sculpture garden – tote a book & a coffee to the café near the fountain – you are bound to be blown away by the Rijksmuseum. The Dutch national museum is dedicated to fine arts & history and is impossible to miss from its perch at the head of the Museumplein. Since its founding 200 years ago, the Rijksmuseum has been a true cultural gem for the city.

Museumstraat 1
Monday-Sunday 9am-5pm
+31 20 674 7000

shop. culture.

Stedelijk Museum

If, somehow, you've managed to tire of the Old Master works of the Dutch Golden Age (we certainly think it's impossible) and are jonesing for something a little more modern, head over to Stedelijk Museum. This cool museum highlights modern & contemporary art & design; it also happens to have an incredible museum shop packed with unique, beautiful books. It's just around the corner from the Rijksmuseum & the Van Gogh Museum, so it's easy to soak up a lot of culture in one go.

Museumplein 10
Monday-Sunday 10am-6pm
+31 20 573 2911

"Head to het Stedelijk early Sunday morning, and you'll enjoy an almost private view."

— Stephanie & Maurits

OUD-WEST & DE BAARSJES

A veritable melting pot, Oud-West & De Baarsjes are the best
—always changing & always exciting.

GET TO KNOW OUD-WEST & DE BAARSJES

We could swear that every time we blink, there's a new, "cool" neighbourhood in Amsterdam. What was once a bit out of the way for *echte Amsterdammers* has now become a bustling melting pot chock-full of chic cafés, fun bars, killer bakeries and great restaurants. Oud-West & De Baarsjes butt up against De Jordaan and Westerpark, separated by the snaking lines of the Marnixstraat and the Haarlemmerweg. And while these chill, vibey neighbourhoods are only a quick cycle from Oud-Zuid and Grachtengordel, they have a character all their own.

With the Vondelpark to the south, the Rembrandtpark to the west and the Erasmuspark smack dab in the middle, Oud-West & De Baarsjes are surrounded by greenery. The hodgepodge of vintage shops, outdoor markets and international restaurants really make Oud-West feel like a village, a city within a city. No longer Amsterdam's 'Wild West', this neighbourhood is vibrant, welcoming and getting better by the minute. Skip the hidden treasures of Oud-West & De Baarsjes at your own risk. You'll be missing out. Big time.

Joris Geurts

cover artist of AMSTERDAM the gloobles guide

There's little in the creative realm that Joris hasn't mastered. A life playing and composing music. A storied career as an artist. An appreciation for beauty that runs deep in his veins. Whenever we want tips for something true, something unique, Joris is our very first port of call. And the best thing about Joris (in our opinion, of course)? He created the striking work that graces the cover of this very book. Lucky us. Lucky you!

"Oud-West is one of the most vibrant and constantly changing neighbourhoods in Amsterdam."

Amsterdam is where you had to be as a budding artist. In the early 1980s, I rented a tiny studio on the Jacob van Lennepstraat and later a somewhat larger one in De Baarsjes. The neighbourhoods were in disrepair, fraying at the seams. Two years later, I moved my studio into a sweeping former school building in the heart of Oud-West.

When De Hallen opened in 2015, the neighbourhood finally had a true centre. The former tram depot, built in 1901, is a national monument. Renovated after years of vacancy, today, it is a vibrant hub for media, fashion, culture, craft and cuisine. Oud-West has had new life breathed into it. There are many great spots to eat like the enchanting Bar Strangelove, cinemas like Lab111 and charming but still relatively undiscovered canals to wander. It's no wonder the area has become so popular! Fortunately, the neighbourhood is still a breeding ground for artists and designers, thanks to spaces like the leafy former WG area and the Tetterode building on the Bilderdijkstraat.

Oud-West is one of the most vibrant and constantly changing neighbourhoods in Amsterdam. Oud-West is vital and in motion.

Naiara Sabandar & Zana Josipovic

gloobles curators Oud-West & De Baarsjes

Good taste is hard to come by, but great taste is practically mythological. Whenever we want tips, tricks and inspiration from people with truly excellent taste, Zana & Naiara are our first port of call. The dream team behind Amsterdam's perennial favourite Oficina, Zana & Naiara know what's up in restaurants, interiors and places to rub elbows with the supremely cool.

"Lots of cool new places have opened that have made the neighbourhood more of a destination for both visitors and *Amsterdammers*."

We've both been living and working in or around the neighbourhood for quite some time, so for us, it definitely feels like a special place. Over the last few years, Oud-West and De Baarsjes have changed a lot. They've always been slightly more residential areas, a bit removed from the chaos of the city centre. But in recent years, lots of cool new places have opened that have made the neighbourhood more of a destination for both visitors and *Amsterdammers*.

The neighbourhood has a very local feel, and we wanted to create a place that mirrored that sentiment. Now, Oficina has become another hub in the area, a place where people can gather, drop in and hang out; we have a lot of regulars who come in for breakfast or lunch. We love seeing people from the neighbourhood popping in time and time again.

These days, there are a bunch of great spots that have brought a lot of life and diversity to the area. Friedhats FUKU Café has been around for a while, and it's really a wonderful place. We like going there to grab a coffee or some beans to take home. Another favourite spot is House of Fermentation, a woman-run vegan kimchi shop where you can buy a jar (we even have dishes on the menu that use her kimchi at Oficina) or take a workshop. She's doing really cool things with her kimchis and operates on a zero-waste model, which is pretty cool.

Around the corner, you can find Ulmus Bakkerij; they have great stuff from pastries to bread, and it's definitely a super local, community-focused spot. We tend to cook at our homes a lot, picking up produce from the shops and markets in Oud-West or De Baarsjes. But if we do want to go out, we like somewhere super casual and relaxed like Café l'Affiche. After a long day of work, we want something low-key – just a nice, chill brown café for a beer and a little bite.

And one of the nicest things about being out west is how close you are to "nature" – or what feels like it. We work with De Stadsgroenteboer to source some of the vegetables we use at Oficina. We also like stopping by Fruittuin van West when we make the trip out to the farm; it's a lovely place to hang out. Both spots are wonderful if you want super fresh, super local produce. It's amazing to be able to just hop on your bike and feel like you're out in the countryside in only a few minutes.

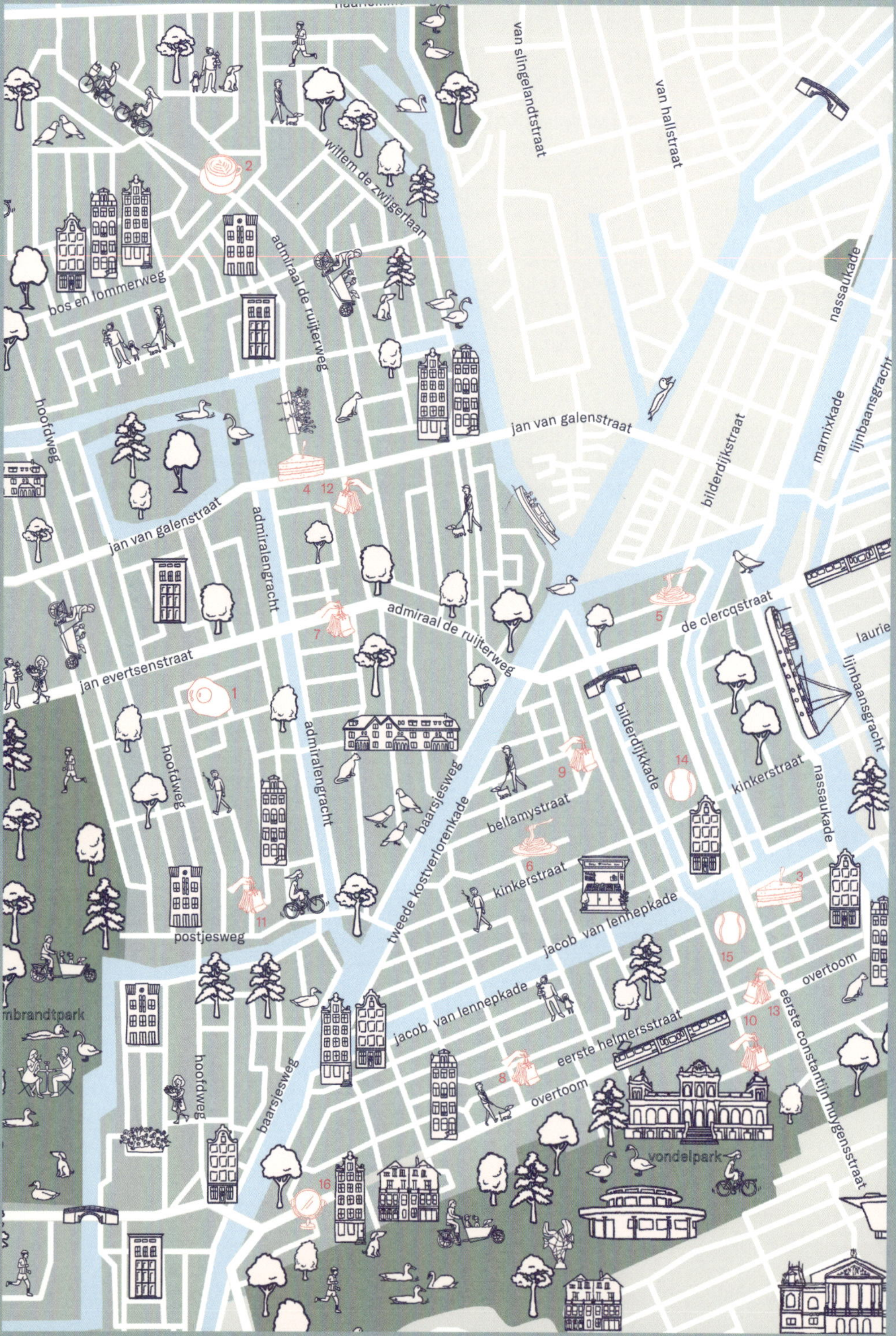
van slingelandtstraat
van hallstraat
willem de zwijgerlaan
admiraal de ruijterweg
bos en lommerweg
nassaukade
hoofdweg
jan van galenstraat
marnixkade
lijnbaansgracht
bilderdijkstraat
jan van galenstraat
admiralengracht
de clercqstraat
admiraal de ruijterweg
jan evertsenstraat
laurie
lijnbaansgracht
bilderdijkkade
admiralengracht
hoofdweg
baarsjesweg
kinkerstraat
nassaukade
bellamystraat
kinkerstraat
tweede kostverlorenkade
jacob van lennepkade
postjesweg
overtoom
jacob van lennepkade
mbrandtpark
eerste helmersstraat
eerste constantijn huygensstraat
overtoom
hoofdweg
baarsjesweg
vondelpark
1
2
3
4
5
6
7
8
9
10
11
12
13
14
15
16

OUD-WEST & DE BAARSJES

get breakfast

breakfast. coffee. takeout. shop.

Ulmus Bakkerij

We are pretty thrilled that there are now so many great places to buy bread in Amsterdam. One that we almost missed—but are very glad we didn't—is Ulmus Bakkerij. The humble, unassuming neighbour of a more Instagrammed but arguably equally good bakery, Ulmus is a real gem. The breads have a fantastic crust, and the pastries (think sticky cardamom buns) are not to be missed.

Cabralstraat 7
Tuesday-Friday 8am-4pm & Saturday 9am-4pm
& Sunday 9am-3pm

get coffee

coffee. takeout.

Friedhats FUKU Café

Don't you ever want to go somewhere that just makes you feel cool? The kind of place where you look around and everyone is stylish and seems to be engaged in super intellectual discussions? Well, FUKU is just such a place. Come here for a dose of cool & a fantastic cup of coffee. Oh, and don't forget about the delicious pastries, homemade granola & natural wine!

Bos en Lommerweg 136
Monday-Friday 8am-4pm & Saturday-Sunday 9am-5pm

get lunch

lunch. drinks. dinner.

Gertrude

Chill & down-to-earth, Gertrude is quintessentially Amsterdam. Though it's new to the dining scene in the city, it feels like one of those places that we've been going to for years. The combination of warm service, a carefully considered wine list & a sun-drenched terrace makes Gertrude an especially lovely place to go for a *heerlijke* bite & a crisp *wijntje*.

Bosboom Toussaintstraat 28h
Monday 5.30pm-1am & Tuesday-Thursday 5.30-10pm
& Friday-Sunday 12-5pm, 5.30-10pm
+31 20 247 0013

breakfast. coffee. lunch.

Oficina

We could never get enough of chef Naiara's creative, craveable concoctions when she was at the helm at T O K I, and things are no different now that she's heading things up at Oficina. She and fellow gloobles friend Zana have teamed up to create what is undoubtedly one of the most popular (and justifiably so) restaurants in the city.

Jan van Galenstraat 147
Thursday-Sunday 10am-5pm

get dinner

"Natural wine, delicious food, funky tunes & a relaxed atmosphere."

— Zuzia

breakfast. coffee. lunch. drinks. dinner. takeout. shop.

café binnenvisser & bakkerij louf

This sweet little brown café is here to prove that the Brits don't have a monopoly on the intimate gastropub. Though this is a traditional drinking establishment that's perfect for slinging back a few beers, they are also pumping out fresh, delicious dishes to accompany their unexpectedly good bottles of natural wine. If you're a carnivore, be sure to order the bone marrow. We implore you.

Bilderdijkstraat 36 & 38
café binnenvisser: Monday-Thursday 6pm-12am
& Friday-Saturday 5.30pm-1am & Sunday 6pm-12am
bakkerij louf: Monday-Sunday 8am-3pm

drinks. dinner.

Petit Péché

The food is solid here, sure, but the reason we really love Petit Péché is the vibe. The space is warm and beautiful, and the staff is not just knowledgeable and friendly but also almost obscenely good looking. Pop by when things are just a little too full? Head over to their sister restaurant, Café Beurre.

Nicolaas Beetsstraat 51
Wednesday-Thursday 6pm-12am & Friday-Saturday 6pm-1am
+31 61 429 1559

get shopping

takeout. shop

Fort Negen & Fort Negen Sandwich Bar

If there's one thing we learned during the pandemic, it's that we should give up our dreams of amateur sourdough and leave the bread baking to the pros. And when we want to grab a loaf that puts our homemade loaves to shame, Fort Negen is pretty much always top of our list. If you're knocking around on Saturday, we highly recommend snagging one of their homemade frozen custard on a croissant cone. For something more substantive, hop next door to grab an aubergine schnitzel sandwich or the goat cheese wrap.

Jan Evertsenstraat 31 & 37h
Fort Negen: Monday-Saturday 8am-6pm & Sunday 8am-4pm
Sandwich Bar: Wednesday-Saturday 11am-3pm
+31 62 426 7713

"Get your hands on a big paper bag containing the best bread in Amsterdam."

— Athena

coffee. takeout. shop.

levain et le vin

For all of the *broodjes* we eat here in Amsterdam, there used to be surprisingly few really fantastic bakeries. But fear not: there is one that may be better than any Parisian boulangerie. levain et le vin is a wonderful bakery & wine shop that sells gorgeous loaves of sourdough bread & exciting, unusual natural wines. Did we mention it's adorable too?

Jan Pieter Heijestraat 168
Tuesday-Thursday 8.30am-5pm & Friday 8.30am-6pm
& Saturday-Sunday 10am-5pm

takeout. shop.

Miuz Gelato Artigianale

One of our favourite things to serve up at the end of a successful dinner party is affogato. And where do we go to get that gelato for our go-to sweet treat? Miuz. This dreamy gelateria is a respite from the busy Overtoom, whether you're grabbing a cone to-go or taking a tub home for later.

Overtoom 117
Monday-Sunday 12-10pm
+31 20 785 2994

shop.

RAE Blooms

RAE is not your typical florist. Run by Australian transplant Ariella Hill, this floral studio feels as if it could only exist in a Roald Dahl story or a Tim Burton film. But, lucky for us, it is a real-life brick-and-mortar shop in the heart of Oud-West. There is no bloom too wild or branch too weird for RAE. Tiny bananas. Cerulean petals. Here, anything goes.

Postjesweg 66
Thursday-Friday 12-6.30pm & Saturday 11-6pm
+31 68 753 2767

shop.

ted.

No colour left behind. No curve not explored. ted. is a place where fun, funk and whimsy rule. This creative space is a home for contemporary art & design, where photographers can shoot and interior lovers will drool. Daphne Weersink, the mastermind behind the shop, has amassed an impressive collection of unique mid-century modern and vintage furniture that design fiends can rent or buy at ted.

Jan van Galenstraat 143
open by appointment
+31 62 386 2222

shop.

Vleck

These days, it's pretty easy to find a great spot to pick up a bottle of natural wine or two, and we must say we're pretty thrilled about that. But just a few years ago, it was a near impossible feat unless you knew about OG natural wine shop Vleck. Today, this wholesaler & importer is still leading the charge in wonderful, exciting natural wines.

Eerste Helmerstraat 63hs
Monday 2-7pm & Tuesday-Friday 10.30am-7pm
& Saturday 10am-5.30pm
+31 20 683 5980

get active

activity.

Saints & Stars – Oud-West

If you've flipped through this book a bit, you likely noticed quite a few cool, boutique fitness studios. While we don't want to spoil you for choice, we wanted to slip another in the list because we think it's really something special. Saints & Stars is not only a killer 50-minute boxing workout but also one of the chicest gyms we've ever seen. We dare you not to snap a photo!

Tweede Constantijn Huygensstraat 41
Monday-Thursday 7am-9.30pm & Friday 7am-7.30pm
& Saturday 7.30am-5.30pm & Sunday 8.30am-5.30pm
+31 20 891 5549

get beautiful

beauty.

An Chi Massage Lounge

Get ready to take a breath & relax, as this traditional healing massage parlour wants you to focus on energy flow and slowing down. Once you arrive at An Chi Massage Lounge, you'll feel truly transported, as it is like no other place in Amsterdam. Their tailor-made treatments are inspired by different spiritual schools of thought (think Buddhism, Taoism & Confucianism), so choose what resonates with you most.

Overtoom 522h
Monday-Sunday 10am-10pm
+31 20 363 6196

If you have a little more time to explore, head out of Amsterdam and really get to know the Netherlands.

VENTURING OUT OF THE CITY

So, you've ticked off all your must-sees in the city, you've still got two days left of your trip and you're starting to get restless. What's a person to do? Why, get out of the city, of course! While we absolutely adore Amsterdam and can hardly imagine that anyone would want to leave, we understand that little adventurous itch that creeps up every now & again.

Luckily, the Netherlands is a small country, and Amsterdam is well placed for exploration. Feeling like fresh air & a dip in the sea? Hop in the car and head to Waterleidingduinen & Fosfor. In the mood for some culture? Head to Centraal Station and grab a train to Haarlem to visit the Teylers Museum & the Frans Hals Museum. No matter the mood, we know you'll find something here to tickle your fancy. Just promise us you'll come back to Amsterdam soon!

Groningen
2
13
5
12
3
1
Haarlem
10
Amsterdam
8
7
9
6
Den Haag
Utrecht
4
Arnhem
11
Rotterdam
Breda
Tilburg
Eindhoven
Maastricht

VENTURING OUT OF THE CITY

coffee. drinks. activity.

Amsterdamse Waterleidingduinen

We don't think we can accurately describe how transportive a visit to Waterleidingduinen is, so we have to insist that you check it out yourself. A walk through this stunning nature park will have you feeling as if you're really on safari. After a scenic hike, check out bohemian beach club Fosfor for a coffee or drink before diving into the sea.

Vogelenzangseduinweg 2, Vogelenzang
open from dawn to dusk

activity. culture.

Broek in Waterland

With many of the houses in this tiny, adorable village built before 1850, it's an enchanting place to spend a sunny afternoon. It is so charming & well-manicured that French visitors in the 18th century referred to Broek in Waterland as *le temple de la propreté hollandaise*. Head here by bike when you're ready to escape the city and see something new.

sleep. breakfast. coffee. lunch. drinks. dinner. activity.

De Durgerdam

Waking up in the charming, briny coastal village of Durgerdam, you'll have a hard time believing that the fervent cyclists and "green-seeking" tourists of Amsterdam are just around the corner. De Durgerdam is a luxurious boutique hotel that allows you to step out of the chaos of the city and into a 17th-century Flemish painting.

Durgerdammerdijk 73, Amsterdam
+31 20 218 4463

breakfast. coffee. lunch. shop. activity.

De Lindenhoff Marché

Amsterdam has a few nice supermarkets – we like Ekoplaza & Landmarkt – but to get really fresh stuff you either have to hit up the weekly markets or head out on a little jaunt from the city to De Lindenhoff Marché. This amazing farm shop & market is a fab place to pick up top-quality meat & vegetables. Before you head home, sit down for a delicious lunch while the kids get up close & personal with the adorable farm animals.

Rijksstraatweg 21, Baambrugge
Thursday-Friday 9.30am-5.30pm & Saturday 9.30am-4.30pm
+31 294 291 071

coffee. activity. culture.

Haarlem

Just a short train ride from Amsterdam, Haarlem is one of the sweetest towns around. Spend the day meandering through the charming streets, taking in the fantastic architecture. It's the perfect day trip to get a feel for how the Dutchies really live. While you're there, don't miss the Teylers Museum or the Frans Hals Museum. They are definite must-sees. Grab a coffee at Jules and lunch at PIP Deli before heading back to the capital.

activity. culture.

Kröller-Müller Museum

Nestled in the Hoge Veluwe National Park in Otterlo, about 2 hours southeast of Amsterdam, Kröller-Müller is an incredible national art museum & sculpture garden. Founded by prolific art collector Helene Kröller-Müller in 1938, the museum is home to the second largest collection of paintings by Vincent van Gogh after the Van Gogh Museum, including a fantastic version of *The Potato Eaters*.

Houtkampweg 6, Otterlo
Monday 12-5pm & Tuesday-Sunday 10am-5pm
+31 318 591 241

culture.

Kunstmuseum Den Haag

Founded in 1866, Kunstmuseum Den Haag is one of the best places in the Netherlands to see modern and contemporary art. The sprawling museum houses a collection of about 165,000 works, including pieces from artists like Pablo Picasso, Frank Stella, Egon Schiele, Claude Monet and Edgar Degas. Don't miss our favourite piece in the museum: Piet Mondrian's last work, *Victory Boogie-Woogie*.

Stadhouderslaan 41, 2517 HV Den Haag
Tuesday-Sunday 10am-5pm
+31 70 338 1111

coffee. culture.

Museum Beelden aan Zee

While there are innumerable inspiring museums in the Netherlands—Het Rijks, Het Stedelijk, Kröller Müller—there is only one that specialises in sculpture: Museum Beelden aan Zee. Founded in 1994 by collectors Theo and Lida Scholten, the museum shows a beautiful collection of both international and Dutch sculpture in a stunning villa by the sea.

Harteveltstraat 1
Tuesday-Sunday 10am-5pm
+31 70 358 5857

coffee. lunch. activity. culture.

Museum Voorlinden

If you can gear yourself up to take the train (or a car if you're bold) out to Wassenaar, you can spend no more glorious an afternoon than one studying the gorgeous collection at Museum Voorlinden. Focusing on both modern & contemporary art, the museum houses the Caldic Collection, the largest private art collection in the Netherlands. The design & architecture are partially inspired by the Danish Louisiana Museum of Modern Art.

Buurtweg 90, Wassenaar
Monday-Sunday 11am-5pm
+31 70 512 1660

activity. culture.

Naarden Vesting

Known for its famous 'star fort' grid resembling a giant snowflake, Naarden is a cute town east of Amsterdam that is one of the most well-preserved fortified towns in all of Europe. Pop into the Grote Kerk, one of the oldest churches in the country, and be sure to check out the Vestingmuseum before getting lost in the winding streets of the town or enjoying a scenic walk around the fortress.

Sabine Marcelis & Paul Cournet

curators for Rotterdam

To say that Sabine and Paul have great taste is an understatement of the highest order. A Dutch designer and a French architect respectively, the pair are always on the hunt for inspiring exhibitions, beautiful buildings and covetable design wherever they go—especially at home in Rotterdam. Culture certainly leads their travels, but they're enchanted by true, wild nature too. And thankfully, they're 100% on the same page when it comes to where they go and what they do. Just so long as it takes them outside of routine, outside of themselves and into somewhere new, somewhere that moves them.

"It's Dutch in a very progressive way—at the forefront of innovation, welcoming and international."

Rotterdam is a multicultural, diverse city where you can actually feel very welcome as a foreigner. I arrived here in 2010 as a young architect for an internship at MA, a big architecture firm, but I actually arrived in the Netherlands in the early 2000s for my undergrad. The Netherlands has always been a great place to be when it comes to architecture and culture in Europe, so when I had the chance to come here, it was very exciting.

Rotterdam is still a bit of an underdog; it's underrated, in my opinion. But as it is an underdog, the city has a lot of freedom. Rotterdam was destroyed during the Second World War, but this actually made a lot of space for architects to come up with new ideas. There was a lot of room for exploration and experimentation.

After I arrived here over a decade ago, it very quickly felt like home. And in the past 10 years, the city has changed a lot. Restaurants, culture, going out. It used to be quite rough—and it still is a little rough—but it has a very good edge to it. It's a city that has a lot to offer for locals and for people who come for a weekend or for a night. There is so much to do here in terms of museums, festivals and dining. It's wonderful because it's a harbour and a haven for different cultures. There is not just one identity. The city has many identities. If you know what you're looking for, no matter how specific, you can certainly find it in Rotterdam.

It's a city that has never tried to be anything. It has no need to keep up with its own standards or expectations. It is what it is; it simply exists. It's Dutch in a very progressive way—at the forefront of innovation, welcoming and international.

For me, the icon of Rotterdam is the Van Nelle Factory, which is this amazing, modern building that was initially built for a tea and coffee company. Now, it's a kind of cultural hub. It has this really industrial past but is the perfect representation of the city and its identity.

Rotterdam is quite a small city at its core, so it's easy to zip around and go out for dinner or see friends. Everyone you know lives about 10 minutes from each other. My partner Sabine and I have a small child, so we love hopping on our bikes and going to see an exhibition or heading to the food market in Blaak. It's this great weekend food market that has incredible fish and all kinds of super Dutch products.

In the next few years, I imagine Rotterdam will start to get more and more attention both in the Netherlands and internationally. I think it's going to become a big hotspot, especially as people become tired of hectic, big city life, where things feel a bit more generic. But what I hope is that Rotterdam stays true to itself and doesn't forget its past. I hope it remains authentic. That it remains Rotterdam.

Sophia van den Hoek

photographer of AMSTERDAM the gloobles guide

Most people eat with their eyes, and it's never been truer for anyone than the fantastically talented photographer, Sophia van den Hoek. This voracious eater loves to uncover anywhere and everywhere that's good to eat, whether it's a hole in the wall or a temple of high gastronomy. This Dutch talent has an eye for all things beautiful and delicious.

"Rotterdam. My city. Full of creativity, a progressive vibe and surprises."

Can you call me a real Rotterdammer? I've been living in this city for over half my life, so I think that I finally qualify. There's this undefinable love you can have for a place. Pride or the spirit of a city that reconstructed itself, becoming what may seem like a bustling metropolis but is really nothing more than a big village. With all the travelling I do, Rotterdam is my perfect home base.

It might not be the prettiest or most charming city at first sight, but once it's got you in its grip, it's pretty difficult to replace. In the Netherlands, there's no other city in which I'd rather live. Rotterdam is home to more than 170 different nationalities. It is this very mix that I love. I love the contrasts, the surprises and the ability to experience the world in my big village.

Rotterdam West has my heart, from my favourite kitschy Indian restaurant just five minutes from my apartment to my local coffee bar. When I feel compelled to leave the neighbourhood, I'll go to Oogstmarkt to pick up groceries and maybe have a drink and a bite. However, I rarely feel the need to leave. The prettiest streets in the city criss-cross the rougher sides of the city, ensuring things never get boring. On a lazy (preferably sunny) weekend, I'll have a walk through Euromast Park. Afterwards, I'll pop into Depot Rotterdam for a bit of culture or De Ballentent for an unpretentious gehaktbal & a beer. There's nothing Instagrammable here, but it's the perfect place to experience the old-fashioned harbour spirit.

If I don't head to Renilde for dinner afterwards (the views of the city are really something), then I'll probably go to one of my favourite restaurants in town: Bar Berta. It's conveniently rolling distance from my apartment, which is ideal, as they have a great little list of natural wines and tapas that are to die for. If I've still got steam after dinner, I love taking a water taxi to Putaine, a floating restaurant with excellent cocktails and beautiful dishes.

Rotterdam. My city. Full of creativity, a progressive vibe and surprises. It might not be love at first sight for most people, and it may not be as easy on the eyes as our capital. But I'd urge you: broaden your view, and you'll be welcomed with open arms. And you will embrace Rotterdam in yours, too.

breakfast. coffee. lunch. drinks. dinner. activity. culture.

Rotterdam

In recent years, Amsterdam has become pretty polished, pretty posh. Rotterdam, on the other hand, is only just now beginning to have its renaissance, and we are here for it. This second city is not one that should be overlooked. We love its striking, angular buildings, burgeoning contemporary art scene & world-class Kunsthal. So hop on the train and spend the hour plotting points – MECCA, Man Met Bril Koffie, Studio Unfolded, Bar Berta, & Restaurant Tres – to visit using Google Maps.

lunch. dinner. activity.

Vuurtoreneiland

There's something truly magical about Vuurtoreneiland. Although it can be difficult to get a reservation, it's totally worth the effort. After boarding a boat (complete with snacks & drinks), you arrive to a stunning private island that's home to a lighthouse and a wonderful restaurant serving a thoughtful set menu & gorgeous wines. Before you settle in for your meal, spend a few minutes exploring the island in the hopes of catching sight of the sweet lambs scampering across the grass.

departure across The Hoxton, Lloyd Amsterdam on Veemkade: Tuesday-Saturday 6.15-11.45pm & Sunday 3.15-8.30pm
+31 20 362 1664

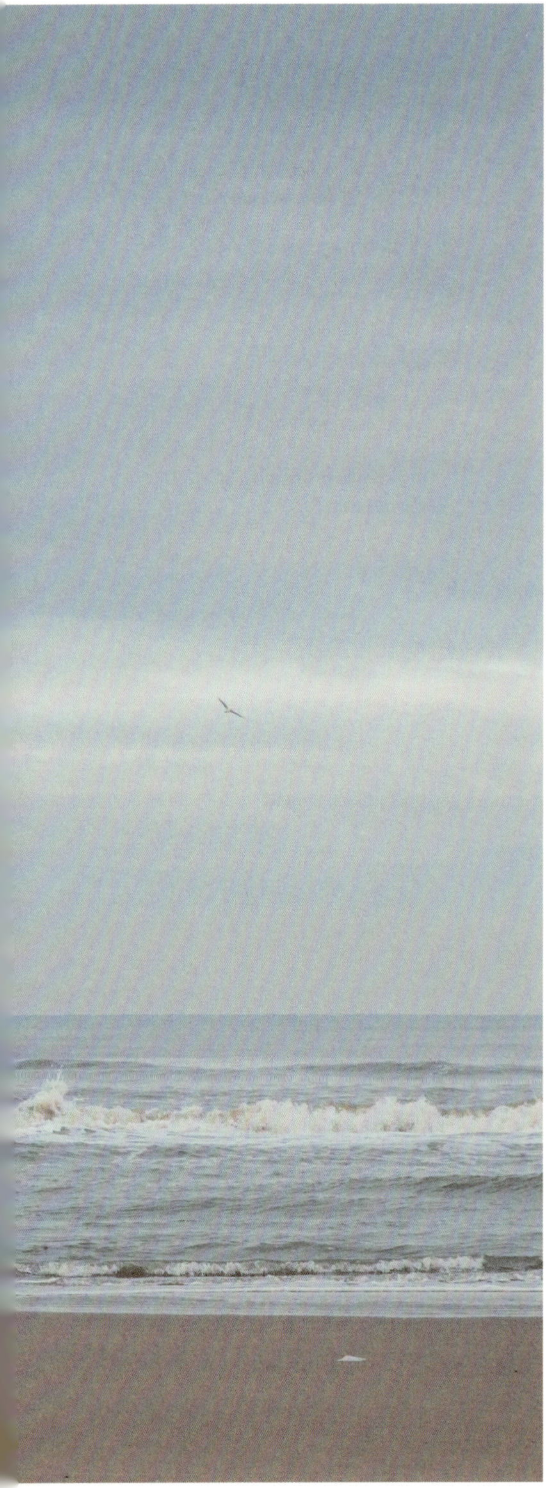

breakfast. coffee. lunch. drinks. dinner. activity.

Zandvoort & Bloemendaal aan Zee

In the mood for a beach day? A little bit of sand & sun? In about half an hour, you'll be soaking up some rays at either Zandvoort or Bloemendaal. Who needs the South of France? If you go, you absolutely must check out bohemian beach shack Fosfor in Zandvoort or sleek & chic beach club Republiek in Bloemendaal. The world is your oyster!

Republiek Bloemendaal (Zeeweg 94 in Bloemendaal): Monday-Sunday 9am-11pm
Fosfor (Zuidstrand 7 in Zandvoort): Monday 12-10pm & Tuesday-Sunday 9.30am-10pm

Can't quite decide what to do? Let us make things easy with one of our dreamy strolls or cycles.

strolls & cycles: routes for exploring the city

You could certainly wind your way through the city on trams or in cabs, but we're of the mind that you can only get a real feel for Amsterdam when you use your feet. Whether by foot or by bike, you'll get to know the ins & outs of town like a real local.

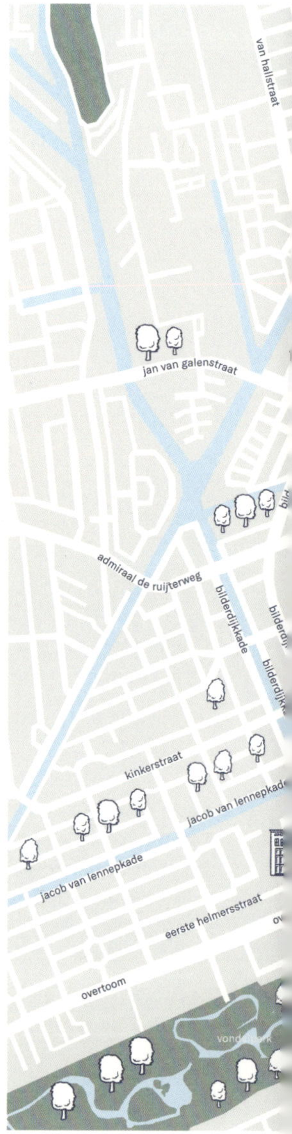

Amsterdam for our artsy friends

Wake up with the sun & settle in at Café de Pels (1) with a book in hand. On the menu? A flaky croissant, a glass of orange juice (squeezed in-house) and, of course, a strong cup of coffee. After breakfast, stop by GRIMM Gallery (2), one of the nicest contemporary galleries in the city, and Anouk Beerents (3), a shop dedicated to vintage mirrors. Once you are amply inspired, continue your stroll past Rika Studios (4), a chic boutique brimming with jewellery & art, women's fashion and niche fragrances. Head over to our favourite book & magazine shop, Athenaeum (5) and spend a few minutes (or a few hours) flipping through photobooks and special magazines. Wind your way over to De Collectie Six (6) for one of the most special museum experiences around. Art historians lead an hour-long tour through the stunning historic house, drawing your eye to wonders of the family's collection. Pass by FlowerLovesMe (7) for an artful bouquet of fresh flowers or a lovely potted orchid. But don't get distracted, as a delicious lunch awaits you at CARMEN (8). Order one of their bright seasonal dishes with a glass of wine or a lapsang tea. If the weather is nice, grab a seat outside on the tiny terrace or in the garden. Once you've had your fill, find your way to Back to Black (9). Grab a coffee (and a piece of banana bread) to-go and head to the 'Louvre of the Netherlands', the Rijksmuseum (10). Take in iconic works by Rembrandt, Vermeer and Frans Hals, as well as stunning period

furniture and ceramics. While we love some of the more blockbuster works, we are completely enamoured by *Winterlandschap met ijsvermaak* by Hendrick Avercamp. It's wise to book a ticket in advance. If you're not totally exhausted, head to the Stedelijk Museum (11) next door to see the permanent collection or one of the daring temporary exhibitions. Oh, and don't forget to grab a free audio tour (available in 6 languages) to help with future dinner party trivia. End your artsy route at Stedelijk bookshop (12) to find a chic souvenir or nice present to tote home.

Make use of a free audio tour to help with future dinner party trivia.

Amsterdam for our history buff friends

Start the day on a healthy yet supremely delicious note with breakfast at bakkerij louf (1). Once you've finished your cheese & mustard croissant and espresso, cycle or hop on the tram for a short ride to the Anne Frank House (2). Even if you don't go inside for a visit, it's incredibly moving to see the place where Anne and her family sheltered from the nazis during the Holocaust. From there, find your way to De Oude Kerk, Amsterdam's oldest building and youngest art institute. Founded in the early 1200s, this church simply pulsates with history. Meander over to the Museum van Loon (3), a gorgeous canal-side house that provides a window into life during the Golden Age. Willem van Loon was one of the founding members of the V.O.C. (the Dutch East India Company), so you will find exotic artefacts & intriguing décor throughout the house. Don't miss the gorgeous garden that separates the main house from the restored *koetshuis* (coach house), which is still in use today. Walk past the gorgeous bridge de Magere Brug (4) to the Jewish quarter and pay a visit to the majestic Portuguese Synagogue (5). If you're lucky, you may stumble into one of their spectacular concerts where hundreds of candles the 17th-century interior. On your way to lunch, stop by the Monument to Jewish Resistance (6). Treat yourself to a riot of seafood at Bistro de la Mer (7). Oysters. Mussels. Eel carbonara. Ooof–heaven! After lunch, trot over to legendary jewellery shop Lyppens (8). You'll spend hours perusing several floors of beautiful silverware, jewellery & stones, but keep an eye on that watch, as there's no time to waste if you want to get to Begijnhof (9),

one of the oldest *hofjes* in Amsterdam. Ready to rumble? Head to Onze Lieve Heer op Solder (10) with its stunning hidden Catholic church. The house unfolds like a storybook, with each room telling a different tale. Rest your feet & ruminate on your busy day with fresh beer from the tap at the former keeper's cottage, the wonky little pub Café de Sluyswacht (11). Wind down with a delicious Dutch dinner in one of Amsterdam's original neighbourhoods at the local haunt Gebroeders Hartering (12), run by brothers Paul & Niek. Still have a little steam left? One final *biertje* at Café 't Hooischip (13), a quintessential old-school brown café, is in order. *Proost!*

Oysters. Mussels.
Eel carbonara.
Ooof – heaven!

Amsterdam for our stylish friends

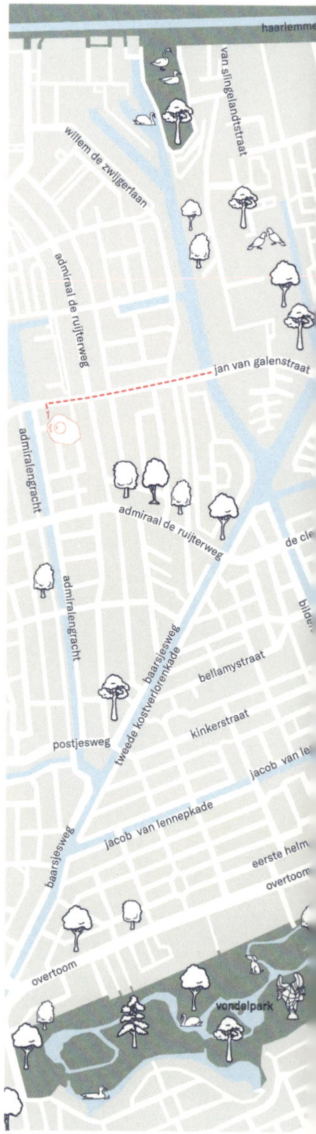

Start the day on a healthy yet supremely delicious note with breakfast at Oficina (1). Once you've finished your Hokkaido pumpkin toast and hojicha latte, grab your bike or hop on the tram for a short ride to Artist Lab (2) for a beautiful manicure. Spring for the BIAB. It has the same sleek look as traditional gel but is far better for your nails. Painted and ready to go? Find your way to FOAM (3), a fabulous photography museum that exhibits both emerging artists and photography stalwarts like Helmut Newton & Diane Arbus. Zip over to trendy optician Azijnman (4) for a fashionable new pair of specs on your way to Assort (5), where you can get a fresh, sleek haircut by the team of talented Japanese stylists. Naturally, lunch should be as chic as you are, so we recommend heading to Marie (6) in De l'Europe. After an indulgent lunch, pick up some cool pieces at Cowboys

to Catwalk (7) and Azzuro Due (8). Looking good goes beyond what you're wearing, so we highly recommend a stop at Skins Cosmetics (9) to stock up on glow-inducing essentials. End your day as stylishly as you began with a fab glass of natural wine at café twee prinsen (10) before rubbing elbows with some of Amsterdam's most fashionable folk (and digging into beautifully plated dishes) at Café de Klepel (11) or Calisto (12).

Naturally, lunch should be as chic as you are, so we recommend heading to Marie in De l'Europe.

Amsterdam for our hungriest friends

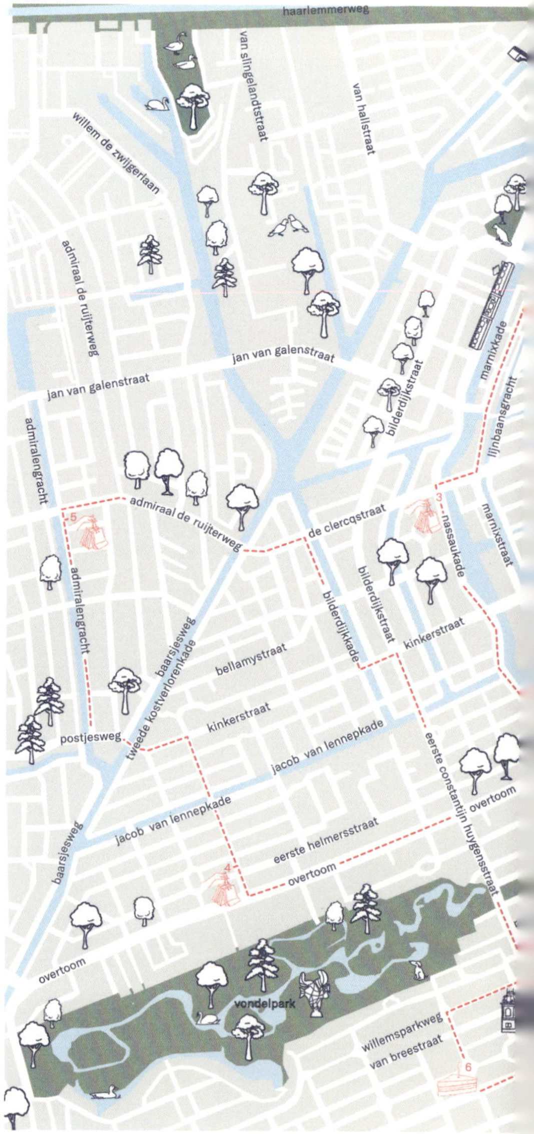

Got your bike? Good! You're ready to go. Since it's Saturday, the best place to begin is De Noordermarkt (1), where you can pick up all the fresh, organic goods you need to cook throughout the upcoming week. The fresh goat cheese & homemade pesto are undeniably good, so be sure to save a little room in your bike basket next to your kohlrabi, kale and corn. Get there a little before the market opens (at 9am) and order a slice of the iconic homemade apple pie from Winkel 43 (2). The lines tend to snake around the corner later in the day, so it's best to get there early. By the time you've finished your pie, the market will be in full swing. When your market bag is full to the brim, find your way to our favourite cheese shop Fromagerie Abraham Kef (3) and stock up on exciting, unusual cheeses. Ask them to vacuum pack them so you can keep them longer (though good cheese never lasts long in our households). But what is cheese without good bread- or wine for that matter? The natural next step is natural wine from levain et le vin (4) & fresh bread from Fort Negen (5). If you, like us, simply cannot wait until you get home, grab a seat on their bench outside and tuck into a bun & a good cup of coffee. By this point, you'll probably be ready to move again, so hop on your bike and cycle through the lush, green & lively Vondelpark on your way to the ZuiderMRKT (6) for a delicious organic lunch from one of the stalls. Once

you've fuelled up, wind your way to Patisserie Holtkamp (7) to buy some beautiful pastries or their legendary garnalen kroket. After all, you can never have enough carbs. Swing by the cookbook shop Mevrouw Hamersma Kookboekwinkel (8) on your way to Bakkerij Mater (9) for some whole-grain, regenerative, organic bread (again, carbs!). Continue the culinary whirlwind and pick up some wine at Glouglou (10) and some aperitivi at Casa del Gusto (11). Snag a bag or two of freshly roasted coffee beans at Rum Baba (12). As we know just how draining stocking your pantry can get, we highly recommend stopping in for a glass or two and maybe even a little dinner at 4850 (13) at the end of the day.

Got your bike? Good!
You're ready to go.

Amsterdam for our friends with kids

Dignita Hoftuin (1) is a hidden oasis that's perfect for enjoying a relaxed breakfast with kids. There's a sweet little corner brimming with toys, and, if the weather is good, the kids can scoop up a toy or two and head out to the lawn to play. The food is delicious, with tons of options for little ones. After breakfast, toddle over to ARTIS (2), the oldest zoo in the Netherlands. With more than 6000 animals, it's the ideal place to spend a few hours with children. As long as everyone–both tall & small–is still up for a stroll, continue on your route to the Oosterpark (3), where there is enough space to let the children run free and a big playground should they need a bit more entertainment. By now, we'd guess the whole family has worked up quite an appetite, so a relaxing lunch surrounded by lush greenery at the Hortus Botanicus (4) is just

what you need. Afterwards, pass by Amstelveld (5) to let the kids burn off a bit of energy; re-up your energy with a coffee on Café Marcella's (6) charming terrace before heading to Khasto in *De Negen Straatjes*. Pick up a few pairs of the cosiest cotton cashmere pyjamas for the little ones and a dreamy robe for you. Swing by Gray Label (7), an adorable shop for children's clothing, afterwards to round off their wee wardrobes. Order an Uber to get to the family-friendly restaurant Café Restaurant Amsterdam (8). If it's too drizzly for all the outdoor activities, you can never go wrong with a (covered) canal boat tour.

If it's too drizzly for all the outdoor activities, you can never go wrong with a canal tour.

Amsterdam for our party friends

Our true party friends may not be rising with the sun (if they've even gone to bed!), so we wouldn't dare suggest starting the day with breakfast. Instead, a late-and possibly boozy-lunch at Café Restaurant Metro (1) is in order. Hair of the dog, they say! After a few croquettes and a hearty serving of saffron risotto, you'll be ready to check out whichever super cool exhibition is on at the Nxt Museum (2). If you're unlucky enough to have forgotten a chic 'fit for going out but lucky enough to catch WIG ANTHOLOGY (3) on one of their sample sale days, wind your way over to the Zamenhofstraat to pick up a piece or two from Danish designers like MADS NØRGAARD. Finally looking the part, you're ready to re-caffeinate at the EYE Filmmuseum's café (4). Evenings in Noord often creep into the wee hours, so a strong espresso is key. With all that newfound energy, you might be ready for something a little stronger. Hop in one of the elevators at the A'DAM Tower (5) and ride it all the way to the top. Grab a drink to sip as the sun sets over the IJ and all of Amsterdam. But don't linger too long, as there are better places to spend the evening! We can imagine you're pretty hungry by now, so we think something delicious is definitely in order. Fight over slices at Euro Pizza

Restaurant (6) or check out their sister spot Restaurant Europa (7) next door. Either way, you can't go wrong. It's full steam ahead with drinks and excellent people-watching at Skatecafé (8). This vibey spot is one of our faves for a night on the town. Ready to dance? Us, too! Shuffle over to Garage Noord (9) to boogie the night away. And, if you're impressive enough to be last man standing (closing down the club at 7am with the bouncers), a warm crolus (a croissant-bolus hybrid) fresh from the oven at Kometen Brood (10) might be just what the doctor ordered to sustain you for your cycle home.

Ready to dance? Us too! Shuffle on over to Garage Noord to boogie the night away.

notes

notes

find it by category

get active

get beautiful

get creative

get cultured

get groovy

get to work

find it alphabetically

gloobles brings the world a little closer

You could certainly wind your way through the city on trams or in cabs, but we're of the mind that you can only get a real feel for Amsterdam when you use your feet. Whether by foot or by bike, you'll get to know the ins & outs of town like a real local.

the platform
Our platform, gloobles.com, is a self-contained universe for intrepid adventurers and armchair travellers. The consummate resource (and ultimate inspiration!), it's packed with destination guides, themed itineraries and engaging listicles and long-form articles.

the publishing house
Our supremely beautiful, infinitely practical guidebooks give you the lowdown on our favourite cities around the world. With a gloobles guide in your bag, you'll travel like a true insider.

the consultancy
Because we understand travel inside and out (and from pretty much every angle there is), we are a strong partner for hospitality brands.

the bespoke agency
Globetrotters by gloobles brings you unique, bespoke travel experiences. We plan and book exceptional itineraries for astute, aesthetic travellers—no matter where they want to go or what they want to do.

head to **gloobles.com**
for more information →

concept and research
Stephanie van Rappard, Hayley Daen, Hannah Rees-Middleton, Kasia Rachuba, Marlise de Buck
of gloobles

editor-in-chief
Stephanie van Rappard
of gloobles

editorial direction & copy
Hayley Daen
of gloobles

photography
Sophia van den Hoek

cover
Joris Geurts

design
Joost Albronda
of Albronda + Rietstap

illustrations
Solgil Oh
Beatriz Sousa

proofreading
William Shaw

printing
Wilco,
the Netherlands

contributing gloobles friends
Athena de Belder
Carmen Atiyah de Baets &
Joris ter Meulen Swijtink
Eben Badu
Hendrikje Crebolder &
Taco Dibbits
Judith Goudsmit
Jetteke van Lexmond
Julia Khan Anselmo
Lukas Lewandowski
Naiara Sabandar &
Zana Josipovic
Sabine Marcelis &
Paul Cournet
Stephanie Schuitemaker &
Maurits de Boer
Steve Musgrave
Tessa Duste
Yvo van Regteren Altena &
Jort Kelder
Zuzia Batolik

publishing
gloobles
fourth edition - Amsterdam, September 2024

ISBN 978-90-9037557-1
NUR 512

While we strive for utmost precision in every detail, we cannot be held responsible for any inaccuracies, nor for any subsequent loss or damage arising.